DBR
P.O. #000-004-886
10-15-90

INTERNATIONAL
TOURISM
POLICY

INTERNATIONAL
TOURISM
POLICY

David L. Edgell, Sr., Ph.D.

Adjunct Professor

The George Washington University

VNR TOURISM AND COMMERCIAL RECREATION SERIES

VNR Van Nostrand Reinhold
_____ New York

1299

This book is the private work of David L. Edgell, Sr.,
and does not represent the views of the United States
Department of Commerce.

Copyright © 1990 by Van Nostrand Reinhold

Library of Congress Catalog Card Number 90-35693
ISBN 0-442-00251-3

Printed in the United States of America

Van Nostrand Reinhold
115 Fifth Avenue
New York, New York 10003

Van Nostrand Reinhold International Company Limited
11 New Fetter Lane
London EC4P 4EE, England

Van Nostrand Reinhold
480 La Trobe Street
Melbourne, Victoria 3000, Australia

Nelson Canada
1120 Birchmount Road
Scarborough, Ontario M1K 5G4, Canada

16 15 14 13 12 11 10 9 8 7 6 5 4 3 2 1

Library of Congress Cataloging-in-Publication Data

Edgell, David L.
    International tourism policy / by David L. Edgell, Sr.
        p.   cm.—(VNR tourism and commercial recreation series)
    Includes bibliographical references.
    ISBN 0-442-00251-3
    1. Tourist trade and state.   I. Title.   II. Series.
    G155.A1E295   1990
    338.4'791—dc20   90-35693
                                                                   CIP

To my son, Nelson M. Nieto,
and
in memory of my parents,
Mr. and Mrs. John J. Edgell, Sr.

CONTENTS

FOREWORD

Worldwide tourism has grown enormously over the past ten years and it will likely continue to do so through the end of this century. It is a part of an overall shift in the postindustrial economy from the product sector to the service sector. International tourism, developed and promoted in an organized fashion, has a bright future. *International Tourism Policy* presents some policy prescriptions for the orderly growth and development of tourism.

The opportunity that tourism offers for positive economic and social benefits for tomorrow will depend on the decisions being made today. We can plan well for the development of tourism or let it happen haphazardly and hope for the best. If we do not define clear-cut policies and plans at this juncture in the growth of tourism, there may never be another chance. We have a limited environment to work with and much of the environment is already under seige from the many different industrial and technological developments underway. To preserve these resources and elicit favorable benefits for tourism is indeed a challenge. This book provides new information and concepts to help us chart a favorable course for tourism and to meet those challenges over the next several years.

Tourism policy links the planning function and political goals for tourism into a concrete set of guidelines to give us direction as we move ahead. Without such guidance we might find tourism's future considerably less beneficial than we hope. With the information and precepts presented in *International Tourism Policy*, students and professionals will have a complete set of conceptual tools for understanding the myriad factors that make up tourism policy and help insure its growth in positive ways.

ANTONIO ENRIQUEZ SAVIGNAC
Secretary-General
World Tourism Organization

SERIES PREFACE

After the "golden era" of international tourism in the decades following World War II, the global competitive situation became more intense, particularly in the 1970s. As a result, more sophisticated marketing techniques modeled after international business and manufacturing approaches were employed by the tourism industry. However, as the confluence of world forces buffeted tourism over the last decade, it was recognized that more effective policies also need to be developed in order to address tourism's role in world economic and social development within the context of a sustainable environment.

The first part of this book addresses tourism policy as it has developed in the United States. In some respects, international tourism policy development in the United States followed Europe's lead. Many of the policy issues now being addressed by the United States are shared with other developed countries and will soon be experienced by newly industrialized countries. Lessons can be learned by other countries from the experience of the United States.

The second part of this book addresses policy issues and policy development processes that are being utilized by the public and private sectors of tourism. The author recognizes that contemporary tourism policy approaches require us to "think globally and act locally" in a responsible manner. The vital importance of community involvement in the tourism development process is stressed.

The appendix section provides useful references to major policies in the United States and at the international level. These documents clearly cite the need for a more balanced and gradual approach to tourism development. Equivalent attention is given to the environmental and sociocultural impacts of tourism in proper perspective to the more tangible economic benefits and costs.

Policies are needed, particularly at the international level, to reconcile private sector concerns with the public interest. The tourism sector will require improved management of its essential functions, including planning, development, finance, human resource development, reseach, and evaluation.

As one of the first books in the travel and tourism professional reference series, this text provides the policy framework essential to produce optimal benefits for tourist destinations, business enterprises, and the traveler.

DONALD E. HAWKINS, GENERAL EDITOR
Tourism and Commercial Recreation Series
Van Nostrand Reinhold

PREFACE

To many, tourism is thought of only as that activity pursued with one's leisure time. While everyone seems to know something about tourism, the industry basically is poorly understood, and much is taken for granted in travel. A partial reason for this shortcoming is because there have not been in existence tourism policy guidelines that explain and demonstrate to policymakers why they should place special emphasis on the tourism industry as it becomes the largest industry in the world by the twenty-first century. *International Tourism Policy* attempts to fill this void and to address some of the more important present and future tourism policy issues within a global context.

This book deals with the symbiotic ties between the economics of international trade in tourism and the links to related nontrade issues, such as increased benefits from cultural exchanges and the promotion of mutual goodwill, and suggests that increased dialogue on tourism issues must take place. It also seeks to demonstrate that not only does international trade in tourism have an impact on the economy, foreign relations, and social fabric of most countries of the world but its growth potential for the future is so significant that it should capture the policy attention of the world's leaders.

Tourism policy worldwide is in its infancy and needs to be nurtured, understood, and supported. Only recently are we seeing travel and tourism courses and programs of study increasing at colleges and universities. A field of inquiry becomes a serious topic for policy analysis and research only when there is interest and recognition in the subject matter through the writing of articles, books, and documents. For tourism, this status has been a recent phenomenon. Only through creative leadership, innovative research, academic inquiry, industry cooperation, and government recognition will tourism policy find its place in the hierarchy of the world's economic and social policies.

This book has been deliberately kept brief and nontechnical to appeal to a broader readership. The aim of this publication is to provide government policymakers (at all levels), business leaders, university professors, students, managers in the tourism industry, and the general public with an introduction and examination of important policy issues in tourism. In brief, this book explains the role that tourism policy plays in integrating the economic, political, cultural, intellectual, business, and environmental benefits of tourism cohesively with people, destinations, and countries in order to improve the global quality of life and provide a foundation for peace and prosperity.

ACKNOWLEDGMENTS

In the course of writing this book, I received much encouragement, help, support, comments, and knowledge from so many different individuals that it would take a full chapter to acknowledge just the names and some of their contributions to my thinking on tourism policy. However, there is one person who has influenced my thinking considerably on broad policy questions (including tourism), who has freely given me his time and advice, who has encouraged me to write this book, and who has been a friend in the truest sense of the word. I want to take this opportunity to thank David N. Parker for being that person in my life.

Even though it is not possible to repay my debts to all those individuals who have unselfishly shared their thoughts on tourism policy with me, I do want to mention three individuals who kindly volunteered their time to read, correct, and suggest changes for improving the contents of this book. I therefore gratefully appreciate, thank, acknowledge, and am deeply indebted to the sincere efforts of my friends and cohorts, Jean O'Brien, Eric Peterson, and Hannah Messerli, for their contributions to this book.

The manuscript for this book would not have been possible if it were not for the untiring efforts of my friend and son David L. Edgell, Jr. He sacrificed his winter break from the university, and many weekends after he resumed his studies in the new semester, to devote the necessary time to the typing and managing of the manuscript for producing this book. He assisted me with the initial research, made helpful suggestions as the book progressed, and attempted in every way to make the author aware of the wonderful world of the computer. I am simply unable to express properly my gratitude, appreciation, and thanks for his devotion and unswerving encouragement, under very difficult circumstances, to see me through this project.

Finally, the responsibility for the book—and the blame for any errors or omissions—rests with the author.

1

TOURISM TODAY

> The world is becoming a global village in which people from different continents are made to feel like next door neighbors. In facilitating more authentic social relationships between individuals, tourism can help overcome many real prejudices, and foster new bonds of fraternity. In this sense tourism has become a real force for world peace.
>
> *Pope John Paul II*

International tourism in the twenty-first century will be a major vehicle for fulfilling people's aspirations for a higher quality of life, a part of which will be through "facilitating more authentic social relationships between individuals" and, it is hoped, laying the groundwork for a peaceful society through global touristic contacts. International tourism also has the potential to be one of the most important stimulants for global improvement in the social, cultural, economic, political, and ecological dimensions of future lifestyles. Finally, tourism will be a principal factor for creating greater international understanding and goodwill and a primary ingredient for peace on earth. This supports the author's view that the highest purpose of tourism policy is to integrate the economic, political, cultural, intellectual, and environmental benefits of tourism cohesively with people, destinations, and countries in order to improve the global quality of life and provide a foundation for peace and prosperity. That is what this book is all about.

For example, since Mikhail Gorbachev became General Secretary of the Communist Party of the U.S.S.R., a more peaceful coexistence has developed between the United States and the Soviet Union resulting in increased tourism between these two nations. In 1985, the complete two-way tourism picture between the United States and the Soviet Union began to change dramatically. By 1989 more than 135,000 Americans had visited the Soviet Union and 60,000 Soviets had come to the United States, up from 6,000 in the early 1980s. "Glasnost" (openness) has made a real difference (see Figure 1.1).

As we approach the threshold of the twenty-first century, the dynamic progress that has been made in international tourism will

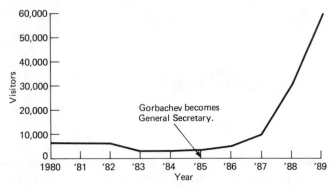

Figure 1.1. Glasnost is real: travel by Soviets to the United States. (Source: USTTA Office of Research)

accelerate even more. This phenomenon is resulting from the fact that the last half of the twentieth century is witnessing tremendous technological changes in transportation and communication, the twin engines that are propelling enormous changes in worldwide tourism. While there have been many turbulences, individual conflicts, and outright wars, the world has been fortunate in avoiding a World War III, especially a nuclear conflict, which, in effect, would have destroyed any progress that has been made in tourism. It has been clear in the past, and will be true in the future, that peace and prosperity are the keys that best open the door to tourism growth. In brief, people in the twenty-first century will look to quality international tourism for creating greater happiness and for improving the human and social aspects of life while at the same time providing opportunities for economic development, job creation, and international trade.

As a way of introduction, this first chapter will summarily describe international tourism within the larger context of the worldwide services economy and set the stage for confronting the policy implications of tourism. There will be a special focus on the United States as the major services economy in the world and as the number-one exporter of trade in tourism. The focus through the "looking glass" in this first chapter will be that international tourism has an optimistic growth future that can best be realized if proper attention to tourism policy is forthcoming.

THE SERVICES REVOLUTION

The nature of the world's productive economic system is changing in a most dramatic way. No longer does the goods-producing economic base dominate. In short, we have entered the services era.

The United States today already is in a "Services Revolution," much as the nation was in an "Agricultural Revolution" over 200 years ago and an "Industrial Revolution" over 100 years ago.[1] This economic transformation is as pervasive and fundamental as was the Industrial Revolution. Since World War II, the United States has moved steadily from a capital-intensive industrial economy based on physical resources to a diversified services economy increasingly based on human resources. Because the country is in the middle of this services "explosion," it is hard to define the parameters. In addition, the services sector, unlike the goods-producing sector, traditionally has not attracted policy attention. Tourism as a service industry has generally received a low priority in policymaking circles. Recently, however, as the economic, political, and social values of tourism have become better recognized and understood, interest in tourism policy has increased considerably. Only time will tell if the current tourism policy thrust will remain as a driving force toward overall improvement in the tourism industry.

OVERVIEW OF THE SERVICES INDUSTRY

It is clear that services trade is a vibrant array of diverse and fast-growing activities such as tourism, engineering, consulting, banking, transportation, motion pictures, insurance, franchising, construction, advertising, and telecommunications. Services trade is now basic to the growth and improved productive system of the United States, even though recognition of its importance in international trade has been slow in coming. Even some of the recent focus on the services sector has evolved as much from the difficulties the United States has had in international trade in goods as from a recognition that this sector is key to the U.S. economy. For example, the trade deficit of the late 1980's caused greater interest in the services sector because the favorable balance of trade in services helped to offset U.S. merchandise trade deficits. The services growth phenomenon is not confined to the United States; it is happening around the world. More important, from a basic international economic perspective, many countries are increasingly recognizing that they must capitalize on their comparative advantage in international trade in services in order to maintain or improve their competitive edge in the global marketplace.[2] Chapter 2 will explain the economic and commercial aspects of tourism within the services context.

Services in International Agreements

The need for recognition of services in international agreements has only recently been gaining attention. This is partly due to a lack of accurate and comprehensive services data and partly because most countries' service sectors are overwhelmingly oriented to the domestic market. In recent years there has been an effort to get barriers to trade in services recognized in an international trade context through the General Agreement on Tariffs and Trade (GATT).[3] Since its inception, the GATT has been devoted exclusively to lowering barriers on goods and commodities. In 1982, the GATT trade ministers finally agreed to study the impact of services trade on member country economies and to examine ways to eliminate service trade restrictions. The effect of these studies and the result of hard negotiating was the inclusion of "Negotiations on Trade in Services" in the GATT *Ministerial Declaration on the Uruguay Round* (see Appendix A) in September 1986, in Punta del Este, Uruguay. In brief, the trade ministers, representing most of the ninety-two member countries of GATT in 1986 (by 1990 there were ninety-seven member countries), decided that Multilateral Trade Negotiations over the next four years would include negotiations on trade in services. This agreement is a historic benchmark for greater policy recognition of trade in services. It has major potential policy implications for international trade in tourism, particularly in the international arena and with respect to the free flow of worldwide tourism. More about GATT and tourism will be discussed in Chapters 3 and 4. Other multilateral organizations are also currently working to reduce trade barriers in tourism, and Chapter 5 will identify some of these organizations.

Services Within the United States

Some potentially encouraging news for the services sector in the United States was the passage of the Trade and Tariff Act of 1984, which established the Service Industries Development Program. This program directs the Secretary of Commerce to seek ways of improving the international competitiveness of U.S. service industries. This trade bill marked the coming of age of service exports, including tourism. The legislation gave the President the same authority to deal with unfair trade practices in areas such as tourism, transportation, insurance, communications, data processing, and financial services as he has in the goods-producing sector.[4] In addition, the Omnibus Trade Act of 1988 mandates that improvements be made in trade data, including services. It remains to be seen if the implementation of these kinds of legislative endeavors will result in improved policy attention for the services sector, including tourism.

The growth of tourism is part of the overall shift in the United States and other highly industrialized nations from prior strength in goods-producing industries to rapid increases in the service industries.[5] This metamorphosis into a service economy took place in the early 1940s when service industry employment topped 50 percent for the first time. As far back as 1968, Victor Fuchs noted:

> The United States is now pioneering in a new state of economic development. During the period following World War II this country became the first nation in which more than half of the employed population is not involved in the production of . . . tangible goods. . . .
>
> The transition from an agricultural to an industrial economy, which began in England and has been repeated in most of the Western world, has been characterized as a revolution. The shift from industrial to service employment, which had advanced furthest in the United States, but is evident in all developed economies, has proceeded more quietly, but it too has implications for society . . . of revolutionary proportions.[6]

Services today account for 67 percent of the gross national product (GNP) in the United States and for more than 50 percent of output produced and consumed in Western Europe and are growing rapidly the world over. The services segment of the U.S. economy employs 75 percent of the work force.[7] The U.S. Department of Labor has predicted that, in the next decade, nine of every ten new jobs created will be in the service industries.

In terms of international trade, services are becoming increasingly important. One of the consistent growth sectors within international trade in services is international tourism. By 1989, over 403 million tourists traveled internationally and spent over $208 billion. Tourism as an international export accounts for nearly 7 percent of total world exports and about 25 percent of international trade in services. The U.S. share of the worldwide market amounted to about $34 billion (excluding transportation receipts).

As a service industry component, tourism makes important contributions to the U.S. economy.[8] Total travel expenditures in the United States, both domestic and international, reached about $350 billion in 1989, or over 6 percent of the GNP. Tourism employed approximately 6 million persons directly or indirectly, or about 6 percent of the total work force.

TOURISM DEFINED

In this book, the term *tourism* is used synonymously with all aspects of travel and tourism unless otherwise specified. With respect to international tourism, this text uses the definitions recommended by the World Tourism Organization as follows:

- **Visitor:** any person visiting a country other than that in which the person usually resides, for any reason other than following an occupation remunerated from within the country visited. This definition covers two classes of visitors: "tourist" and "excursionist."

- **Tourist:** a temporary visitor staying at least twenty-four hours in the country visited, the purpose of whose journey can be classified under one of the following headings: *a.* leisure recreation, holiday, health, study, religion, or sport; and *b.* business, family, mission, or meeting.

- **Excursionist:** a temporary visitor staying less than twenty-four hours in the country visited (including travelers on cruises).

In the preceding section, international tourism was generally included as part of the services industry. To be more specific, tourism, in terms of the balance-of-trade account, is defined as "travel and transportation" and is included in the U.S. trade account as "business services." In the official U.S. trade statistics, under "Types of Business Services in International Trade," there is a separate category referred to as "travel and transportation" with the following definitions:

- **Travel:** services provided to U.S. citizens traveling abroad (U.S. imports) and to foreigners visiting the United States (U.S. exports).

- **Passenger Transportation:** transportation provided by foreign carriers to U.S residents for transportation abroad (U.S. imports) and by U.S. carriers to foreign residents (U.S. exports).[9]

Tourism More Broadly Defined

The late futurist Herman Kahn, in his book *The Next 200 Years* wrote, "It seems reasonable to assume that by the end of the century tourism will be one of the largest industries in the world, if not the largest."[10] What, then, is tourism? Travel, or tourism (*travel* and *tourism* are used interchangeably in this text), means different things to different people. To many individuals and policymakers, travel or tourism is thought of only as an activity pursued with one's leisure time. It is far broader than that, considerably more complicated, and a very significant segment of the world's economy.

A more detailed explanation will follow over the next several chapters. For now, it will suffice to say that tourism has strong links to cultural pursuits, foreign policy initiatives, economic development, and, as stated earlier, provides an opportunity to increase worldwide understanding, mutual goodwill, and peace. The tourism industry includes the buying, selling, and management of services and products (to tourists), which might range from buying hotel rooms to selling souvenirs or managing an airline.

The tourism industry demands the most creative and innovative managers because tourism represents one of the most perishable of the products that exist in the worldwide marketplace. If the hotel rooms, airline seats, or restaurant tables are not filled immediately, they are gone forever—there is no opportunity to put such products in storage or in inventory.

Tourism is also the most wide-ranging industry in the sense that it demands products from other sectors of the economy. For example, the beef and wheat grown in Kansas help feed the international visitors in New York City or Los Angeles. Airplanes must be produced, computer reservation systems developed, and steel and concrete manufactured for hotel construction. The point is that there is no other industry in the economy that is linked to so many diverse and different kinds of products and services as is the tourism industry. In order to plan for and provide rational order to such a diverse and dynamic industry, it is necessary to develop policies to assist the decision makers in this complex industry.

FOUNDATIONS OF TOURISM POLICY

There is no single place in the history of tourism to specifically identify as the sole foundation for tourism policy development. Since the beginning of time, people have traveled for one purpose or another. Because the records of early travel are limited at best to drawings in caves, folk tales and songs, and similar forms of documentation, it is difficult to ascertain what kinds of early policy existed to influence and determine tourism decisions. In short, these sources do not provide enough information to determine if there were policy guidelines or planned development in these early years of tourism.

The Greek civilization was the first to write about tourism. In Plato's *Phaedo* Socrates has this to say: "A great many different countries go to make up our world. . . . It is an enormous place, and we, whose civilization spreads from the river Phasis to the pillars of Hercules, occupy only a small part of it. In other places, there are other men living in countries similar to ours." And certainly the Greek Herodotus (about 480–421 B.C.), a geographer, historian, and traveler, provides us with some interesting information and eyewitness accounts of early travel. But while his journals on travel are fascinating reading, they do not address "policy" issues in tourism. Nor does the interesting information on tourism described by the Roman Sidonius Apollinarius (A.D. 430–489) provide us with a basis for tourism policy analysis.[11]

We have to wait for Marco Polo (1254–1324), the first European to cross the entire continent of Asia and to leave a record of what he saw and heard, to give us some policy direction in tourism. His vivid accounts of travel, written in his book, *The Travels of Marco Polo* (also referred to as Marco Polo's *Description of the World*), allow us to begin to truly understand the early broad ramifications of tourism development and the policies governing tourism at that time. We do know that the world of 700 years ago represented anything but rational order. For example, a foreign traveler was beset with strange customs, chaotic conditions, and very little hospitality. This was the world that Marco Polo entered, in 1254 or shortly thereafter, to record his various travels. If anyone was born to be a traveler and to communicate about its importance in the world social order, it was Marco Polo. His father and uncle were, for the most part, unrecorded world travelers, and Marco Polo early in life had a mental curiosity and a yearning to know about new ideas and faraway places, later leaving a wonderful record of these travels. To pursue the wonders of the world, he was willing to travel by foot, horseback, camel, and boat under some of the most difficult circumstances imaginable. This most famous of all travelers not only endured enormous hardships, he brought back with him new inventions, new customs, new products, and new ways of viewing life. His interactions with the great ruler Kublai Khan and his ability to learn and to transfer knowledge are aptly chronicled in his writings. People read his book, and this stimulated Europe's interest to obtain spices, silks, and other products from the East. And indirectly, it was Marco Polo's great discoveries that eventually caused Columbus, searching for a shorter route to the East, to discover the islands off the coast of the Americas.

In my view, Marco Polo is the cornerstone for the development of tourism policy in that he was the first major traveler to make rational sense out of travel, to give it some direction, and to help us understand how travel impacts on the rest of the world's activities. He identified sociocultural aspects of travel, environmental conditions at the time, and the rustic setting of traveling in sparsely populated areas. And his writings aroused curiosity in others, thus stimulating world travel, which continues to grow to this day.

Modern Tourism Policy

If Marco Polo is the father of tourism policy, we have to wait about 700 years to get to a place in history where we can identify modern tourism policy. It has taken place at different stages in different parts of the world, but if forced to choose one place and time from where today's tourism policy emanated, I would select Europe immediately following World War II. Europe was in economic shambles resulting from the devastation and destruction caused by the war. Every effort was made to seek ways and means to rebuild Europe, and tourism was seized upon as a prime tool for economic development and a potential source for quickly earning badly needed foreign exchange. Despite widespread destruction, most of Europe's ancient and historic treasures survived the war. Americans had the economic means to travel, and Europe was able to get its tourism industry back on track much faster than its industrial production base. Thus, international tourism provided Europe with fresh dollars, which had a broad multiplier effect on the economy (as further explained in Chapter 2.) The Organization for Economic Cooperation and Development (OECD) was established and quickly adopted a tourism policy that became an international model. In brief, Europe began to establish broad tourism policies in the late 1940s and by the 1950s had a well-defined international policy to deal with the tourism product. More will be said about tourism policy in today's world in a later chapter.

International Tourism Policy in the United States

From a policy perspective, the United States did not really understand the intricacies of what was happening in the international tourism arena and the potential positive impact for the U.S. tourism industry until the mid 1950s.[12] In fact, the United States had been encouraging its citizens to travel to Europe as part of its effort to help stimulate the economies of Europe in the reconstruction period. But by about the mid 1950s the United States began to take notice of the large deficit in tourism trade. In 1954 the Commission on Foreign Economic Policy delved lightly into the subject of international travel, but tourism was only one among many important problems of foreign economic policy that were under review and did not, therefore receive the detailed consideration warranted. Finally, under the Mutual Security Act of 1957, President Eisenhower directed that a study of the barriers to international travel, and ways of promoting such travel, be undertaken. This study was completed on April 17, 1958, and submitted as a *Report to the President of the United States* by Clarence B. Randall, Special Assistant to the President. In his transmittal letter to the President, Randall identified some of the policy implications of international tourism and stated:

I hold the strong conviction that tourism has deep significance for the peoples of the modern world, and that the benefits of travel can contribute to the cause of peace through improvement not only in terms of economic advancement but with respect to our political, cultural, and social relationships as well. . . .

The freedom to travel is a dramatic freedom. It is a unique instrument of friendly, peaceful communication among the nations and the peoples of the earth. . . . The United States could exercise no more powerful influence in behalf of peace than to display strong leadership in promoting through travel the interchange of friendly visits among the peoples of the world.[13]

His report, *International Travel,* led to the development of legislation that resulted in the International Travel Act of 1961. This Act established the United States Travel Service (USTS) and mandated that USTS seek to "stimulate and encourage travel to the United States by residents of foreign countries for the purpose of study, culture, recreation, business and other activities as a means of promoting friendly understanding and good will among peoples of foreign countries and the United States."[14]

National Tourism Policy Act of 1981

The next step in the focus on tourism policy in this country began to evolve in 1974. Senate Resolution 347, cosponsored by seventy-one Senators and unanimously agreed to by the Senate on June 24, 1974, authorized the Senate Commerce Committee to undertake a National Tourism Policy Study. The purposes of the study were "to develop legislation and other recommendations to make the Federal role in tourism more effective and responsive to the national interests in tourism, and the needs of the public and private sectors of the industry."[15]

In October 1976, the Committee issued the study's first interim report, *A Conceptual Basis for the National Tourism Policy Study.* This report gave an overview of legislation that affects tourism, tentatively identified the national interests in tourism, and listed some of the problems associated with the Federal role in tourism policy at that time.

In June 1977, a second interim report was issued, the *National Tourism Policy Study Ascertainment Phase.* This report detailed and analyzed input from the tourism and travel industry on the issues, problems, and need of state and local, public and private sectors of the industry, both in general terms and in terms of their specific relationships to Federal agencies and programs.

The last phase, the *National Tourism Policy Study Final Report,* was completed in April 1978. It incorporated findings from the earlier reports and made recommendations for a national tourism policy for the United States.

After considerable discussion of the study, debates in Congress and the executive branch, and consultations with states, cities, and the private sector, a compromise piece of legislation, S.1097, The National Tourism Policy Act, was passed by Congress but vetoed by President Carter on December 24, 1980. It was reintroduced early in 1981 and after Congressional hearings, The National Tourism Policy Act of 1981 was passed by Congress and signed into law by President Reagan on October 16, 1981 (retroactive to October 1, 1981). This Act redefined the national interest in tourism and created the United States Travel and Tourism Administration (USTTA), which replaced the United States Travel Service as the nation's government tourism office.[16]

The principal mission of the USTTA under the Act is to implement broad tourism policy initiatives, to develop travel to the United States from abroad as a stimulus to economic stability and the growth of the U.S. travel industry, to reduce the nation's travel deficit, and to promote friendly understanding and appreciation of the United States abroad. Through the passage and implementation of the Act, the importance of tourism policy within the U.S. Department of Commerce has been elevated. A more comprehensive description of the Act and its policy implications will be presented in a later chapter. For now, it is important to simply recognize that this Act is the most comprehensive identification of tourism policy within the United States.

As this book goes to print, an additional phase in U.S. tourism policy is being considered by Congress. On October 25, 1989, the U.S. Senate introduced S.1791, the Tourism Policy and Export Promotion Act of 1989. This legislation introduces a number of major policy changes that are designed "to assist in the growth of international travel and tourism in the United States, and for other purposes." The U.S. Senate passed this legislation on May 16, 1990. The U.S. House of Representatives introduced H.R. 4369, an almost identical bill to that of the Senate passed S. 1791, on March 22, 1990. The House has not yet enacted this legislation. These pieces of legislation will be the key tourism policy fulcrum for 1990.

While the National Tourism Policy Act and the Tourism Policy and Export Promotion Act are major breakthroughs in gaining recognition for tourism policy in the United States, a lack of awareness and understanding about the significance of tourism in this country still exists. The broad range of economic, political, and social implications for tourism—on both the domestic and international fronts—are yet to be realized. One way of focusing attention on this need for recognition is to examine the larger role that tourism plays in this country, beyond its marketing and promotional aspects.

FUTURE TOURISM POLICY

The tourism industry will be faced with some difficult challenges over the next several years. Technology, whether information technology or new aerospace developments, will heavily impact the tourism industry. The industry will need to develop effective plans to deal with terrorism and other disruptions to the tourism market. New and better approaches in addressing currency fluctuations, whether the latter are due to changes in the value of the dollar, devaluations of currencies, or inflationary conditions, need to be pursued. The way in which the industry responds to these policy questions and new ones as they arise will determine the direction and maturity of tourism policy in the future. These concerns are dealt with in Chapters 6 and 7.

The larger role for tourism policy can only be conceptually understood and substantively analyzed once the philosophical guidelines and practical interests of tourism are investigated and described in a broad contextual framework. The following chapters attempt to sift through the numerous facts and sources of information on the subject of tourism, including a detailed review of its economic and foreign policy implications, while at the same time broaching other important tourism issues. In the process, the book examines the prospects for international travel and tourism for the rest of the century and suggests a focus for international tourism policy in the 1990s.

CONCLUSION

A special category of the service industries is travel and tourism services. In its broadest sense, tourism encompasses all expenditures for goods and services by travelers, including purchases of transportation, lodging, meals, entertainment, souvenirs, travel agency and sightseeing tour services, and personal grooming services.

The full scope of international travel and tourism, therefore, encompasses the output of segments of many industries. The travel "industry" consumes the output of and creates a far-reaching base of wealth for feeder industries such as agriculture, fishing, food processing, brewing, construction, airports, automobiles, and furniture. In addition, tourist activities make use of the services of other industries, such as insurance, credit cards, advertising, and data processing.

Tourism is an economic activity that provides the countries receiving tourists with a dependable source of income and foreign exchange; it creates jobs, reduces unemployment, fosters entrepreneurship, stimulates production of food and local handicrafts, speeds up communications, facilitates cultural exchanges, and contributes to a better understanding of the country and the world at large. The changing dimensions of this vast, expanding industry are bringing into sharper focus concerns over the cultural, ecological, environmental, social, and political consequences of tourism.

Over the next several chapters these aspects of tourism policy and others are presented and discussed in some detail. Through a thorough understanding of tourism's implications, policymakers, planners, and practitioners can help to get the communities involved in the tourism industry at all levels. The more the local community is a part of the decision-making process, the more likely it is that the future of tourism will create positive perceptions.

NOTES

1. "USA and the International Traveler." David L. Edgell. *Tourism Management,* London, December 1983, p. 308.

2. The idea of comparative advantage was first formulated by the classical economist David Ricardo. He reasoned: "If traders were left alone to pursue their own profit by buying in the cheapest and selling in the dearest market, the result of their activities in the long run would be that each country would come to specialize in producing and exporting those commodities in which its comparative advantage, as measured in labor cost, was greatest." Ricardo's concept is an important basis for free trade arguments. Today, economists measure other costs besides labor. As used today, comparative advantage theory simply explains why a country capable of providing a wide range of goods and services at a lower cost than any other country should concentrate on selling that product or service for which its cost advantage is greatest and leave the production of other goods and services, in which it has a positive but lesser cost advantage, to other countries. For a discussion of the principle of comparative advantage, see *Principles of Political Economy and Taxation,* by David Ricardo, Everyman's Library, New York, 1917, Chapter 7; see also *The Theory of International Trade,* by Gottfried Haberler, The Macmillan Company, New York, 1950, and *Pure Theory of International Trade*, by Murray C. Kemp, Prentice-Hall, Inc., Englewood Cliffs, N.J., 1964.

3. For a detailed description and explanation of the policy implications with respect to the General Agreement on Tariffs and Trade, see *Trade*

Talks: America Better Listen! by C. Michael Aho and Jonathan David Aronson, Council on Foreign Relations, New York, 1985.

4. A more complete explanation of the "Trade and Tariff Act of 1984" is contained in the Conference Report, 98th Congress, 2nd Session, U.S. House of Representatives, October 5, 1984. An interesting summary of the impact of this act on tourism can be found in *Travel Industry World Yearbook,* by Somerset Waters, Child and Waters Inc., New York, 1985.

5. *International Business Prospects 1977–1999,* Howard F. Van Zandt (ed.), Chapter Seven, "International Tourism and Travel" (David L. Edgell), Bobbs-Merrill Educational Publishers, Indianapolis, 1978, p. 168.

6. *The Service Economy,* Victor Fuchs, National Bureau of Economic Research, New York, 1968, pp. 1–2.

7. "The Coalition of Service Industries." *The Service Economy,* November 1986, p. 1.

8. A good first explanation of tourism within the services trade is contained in *International Trade in Tourism,* by David L. Edgell, U.S. Department of Commerce, Washington, D.C., October 1985. This presentation of tourism as part of international services is further expanded in *International Tourism Prospects 1987–2000,* by David L. Edgell, U.S. Department of Commerce, Washington, D.C., February 1987. A more recent update of these publications and services information as it relates to tourism can be found in *Charting a Course for International Tourism in the Nineties,* by David L. Edgell, U.S. Department of Commerce, Washington, D.C., February 1990.

9. *United States Trade Performance in 1988*, U.S. Department of Commerce, Washington, D.C., September 1989.

10. *The Next 200 Years,* Herman Kahn, 1976.

11. *History of Tourism.* From the Leisure Arts Ltd. series, "Discovery of Sciences," London, 1966, pp. 9–13.

12. This does not mean that there were not individuals or small groups in the United States suggesting one type of tourism policy or another. Most such actions on the part of such advocates, however, were aimed toward a domestic tourism policy rather than an international one. A good presentation of some of the early thinking along these lines is contained in *The Travel Industry* (2nd ed.), by Chuck Y. Gee, James C. Makens, and Dexter J. L. Choy, published by Van Nostrand Reinhold, New York, 1989, pp. 114–18. A good historical discussion of the evolvement of the National Tourism Policy Act is contained in "Federal Efforts in Tourism: Background and History," presented by John D. Hunt at the meeting on *Travel and Tourism in the U.S.: Prospects and Problems,* Washington, D.C., December 11, 1980. See also "U.S. Government Policy on International Tourism," by David L. Edgell, *Tourism Management,* March 1984.

13. *Report to the President of the United States: International Travel,* Clarence B. Randall, Washington, D.C., April 17, 1958.

14. International Travel Act of 1961, Chapter 31, Section 2122, p. 158.

15. For a clear understanding of the issues discussed and the details of the comprehensive research undertaken, the individual reports of the National Tourism Policy Study should be reviewed.

16. Several articles have been written discussing different aspects of national tourism policy. Some that may be of particular interest are "U.S. Government Policy on International Tourism," *Tourism Management,* Donna F. Tuttle, March 1984, pp. 67–70.

"Developing State Tourism Policies," *Destinations* (American Bus Association), Donna F. Tuttle, January 1985, pp. 30–31.

"Policy Council Coordinates Government Tourism Programs," *Business America,* Donna F. Tuttle, January 7, 1985, p. 36.

SUPPLEMENTAL READINGS

A Conceptual Basis for the National Tourism Policy Study. Warren G. Magnuson, Chairman, Committee on Commerce, and Daniel K. Inouye, Chairman, National Tourism Policy Study for the use of the Committee on Commerce and National Tourism Policy Study. Washington, D.C.: U.S. Government Printing Office, 1976.

Creating Economic Growth and Jobs Through Trade and Tourism. U.S. Government Printing Office, Washington D.C., February 1981.

"Cultural Richness in the U.S. Black Community Offers Great Potential for Tourism Development." David L. Edgell and Bernetta J. Hayes. *Business America.* Washington, D.C. September 26, 1988.

Flying High in Travel. Karen Rubin. John Wiley & Sons, Inc., New York, 1986.

Government Policy in Tourism—Its Economic Importance. David L. Edgell. Paper presented at the Eighth Annual Conference of the Society of Government Economists, Washington, D.C., March 27, 1978.

International Economic Report of the President. Executive Office of the President, Council on International Economic Policy. Washington, D.C.: U.S. Government Printing Office, 1977.

International Travel—International Trade. H. Peter Gray. Heath Lexington Books, Lexington, Mass., 1970.

"Marketing International Tourism: A United States Perspective." David L. Edgell. *T. M. Comenta.* Mexico City, January/February 1989.

Megatrends in International Tourism. Alberto Sessa (ed.). Editrice Agnesotti, Rome, 1987.

National Tourism Policy Study Final Report. Howard W. Cannon and Daniel K. Inouye, Chairmen. Committee on Commerce, Science and Transportation, Washington, D.C.: U.S. Government Printing Office. 1978.

National Tourism Policy Study Ascertainment Phase. Warren G. Magnuson, Chairman, Committee on Commerce, Science and Transportation, and Daniel K. Inouye, Chairman, National Tourism Policy Study for the use of the Committee on Commerce, Science, and Transportation and National Tourism Policy Study. Washington, D.C.: U.S. Government Printing Office, 1977.

The Next 200 Years. Herman Kahn, William Brown, and Leon Martel. William Morrow and Company, Inc., New York, 1976. p. 40.

"An Overall Policy Framework to Restore America's Competitiveness in International Trade in Tourism." David L. Edgell. *Business America.* Washington, D.C. September 26, 1988.

Planning for Tourism Development. Charles E. Gearing, William W. Swart, and Turgut Var. Praeger Publishers, New York, 1976.

Recommendations on International Travel and Tourism, United Nations Publication (E/CONF. 47/18), Rome, August 21–September 3, 1963.

Remarks by David L. Edgell at the National Conference on Tourism Marketing, American Hotel and Motel Association, Kansas City, December 1, 1989.

The Role of Tourism in International Economic Policy. David L. Edgell and Stephen A. Wandner. Joint National ORSA/TIMS Meeting, November 7–9, 1977, Atlanta, Georgia.

"The Role of Tourism in the U.S. Economy," David L. Edgell. Paper presented to the National Economist Club, Washington, D.C., April 1, 1979.

Role of Tourism in the International Economic Policy of the United States. David L. Edgell and Stephen A. Wandner. Paper presented at the Western Economic Association Annual Meeting at Honolulu, June 22, 1978.

Tourism Analysis. Stephen L. J. Smith. John Wiley & Sons, Inc., New York, 1989.

"Tourism: An Economic Development Tool for Black and Minority Chambers of Commerce," David L. Edgell. *Business America.* Washington, D.C., February 15, 1988.

Tourism and the Business Cycle. Stephan Schulmeister. Austrian Institute for Economic Research, Vienna, 1979.

Tourism: Economic, Physical and Social Impacts. Alister Mathieson and Geoffrey Wall. Longman Inc., New York, 1982.

Tourism Management. Salah Wahab. Tourism International Press, London, 1975.

Tourism: Principles, Practices, Philosophies (4th Edition). Robert W. McIntosh and Charles R. Goeldner. Grid Publishing, Inc., Columbus, Ohio, 1984.

"Tourism—The World's Peace Industry," Louis J. D'Amore. *Business Quarterly*. School of Business Administration, The University of Western Ontario, London, Ontario, Canada, 1988.

Tourist Development. Douglas Pearce. Longman, Inc., New York, 1981.

Travel, Tourism, and Hospitality Research. J. R. Brent Ritchie and Charles R. Goeldner (eds). John Wiley & Sons, New York, 1987.

The Travel Trade. L. J. Lickorish and A. G. Kershaw. Practical Press Ltd., London, 1958.

U.S. National Study on Trade in Services. U.S. Government Printing Office, Washington, D.C. 1984.

"U.S. Tourism," David L. Edgell. *Commerce America*. Vol. 11, No. 15, July 18, 1977, pp. 5–7.

CHAPTER

2

INTERNATIONAL TOURISM AS A COMMERCIAL AND ECONOMIC ACTIVITY

"There are yet some other petty things which seem to have reference to this ballance of which the said officers of His Majesties Customs can take to notice, to bring them into accompt: as namely, the expense of travailers."

Thomas Mun—England's Treasure by Foreign Trade, 1620.

Were Thomas Mun alive today, he would not refer so lightly to the expenses of travelers (quoted above as travailers) as "some other petty things" but would instead include the "expense of travailers" as one of the more important entries into the international balance of trade account, or "accompt". The post–World War II years have seen a worldwide increase in leisure time for millions of people in both the developed and developing countries of the world. Indeed, shorter working hours, greater individual prosperity, faster and cheaper travel, and the impact of advanced technology have all helped to make the leisure and travel industry the fastest-growing industry in the world. Today, tourism is indeed an activity of considerable economic importance throughout the entire world. This growing significance of tourism as a source of income and employment, and as a major factor in the balance of payments for many countries, has been attracting increasing attention from governments, regional and local authorities, and others with an interest in economic development. This increased awareness has been slow in coming and, even today, has not for the most part captured the attention of most economic policymakers.[1]

GLOBAL IMPORTANCE

Tourism is an important source of income for most of the countries of the world. Worldwide, international tourist arrivals exceeded 403 million in 1989, and worldwide international tourist receipts (excluding passenger fares) were over $208 billion. About 70 percent of the world's tourism is lodged with the 24 member countries of the Organization for Economic Cooperation and Development. Worldwide expenditures for domestic and international tourism taken together in 1989 were estimated at over $2 trillion. Total worldwide spending for domestic and international travel represented almost 10 percent of the world gross national product. In the United States, tourism represented about 6.7 percent of the U.S. gross national product. Expenditures on travel abroad represented about 7 percent of world trade, placing tourism among the three largest items (alongside oil and motor vehicles) in international trade. In developing countries, tourism represented about one third of the trade in services, and globally, tourism accounted for more than 25 percent of the world's earnings from trade in services. With regard to employment, tourism is estimated to generate jobs worldwide approaching 100 million.[2] Tourism is a major sector of the world economy. When it expands or contracts, nations, their governments, and their people are economically affected. International tourism receipts represent an infusion of fresh hard currency from outside the existing economy and have the same positive impact as other export earnings.

As is indicated, tourism is an important export product in both industrialized and less-developed countries. But the extent to which tourism contributes to a country's foreign exchange earnings varies considerably. In some of the Caribbean nations (particularly countries like the Dominican Republic, Jamaica, and the Bahamas) trade in tourism is very important. For example, tourism accounts for almost 70 percent of foreign exchange earnings in the Bahamas. In Mexico, it is consistently either the second or third most important earner of foreign receipts. For Spain and Italy, tourism is one of the most important components of the economy, and in the United States it is the number-one export, surpassing even agriculture exports in 1988. In 1985, according to International Monetary Fund data, trade in tourism services accounted for almost 42 percent of services in the United States and 44 percent for Italy, 57 percent for Mexico, and 70 percent for Indonesia.[3] The reasons for such uneven distributions of the benefits of tourism vary greatly but partly depend on the comparative advantage of the country as well as its socioeconomic and geopolitical interests in exporting tourism.

For the United States in 1989, international tourist arrivals were approximately 38.7 million, with international tourism receipts of about 43.8 billion (including passenger fares). Expectations for 1990 are that 41 million visitors will come to the United States and spend about $49.7 billion. Expenditures for domestic and international travel services in the United States for 1989 were estimated at over $350 billion and forecasted to be over $374 billion in 1990, based on information from the U.S. Travel Data Center and the United States Travel and Tourism Administration.[4]

Yet, important as tourism is from an economic point of view, it continues to be relatively neglected as an important international economic policy issue. The economic benefits of tourism are often discussed but are seldom fully appreciated. Tourism is an important source of income, foreign exchange receipts, and employment for nearly all countries. The construction and maintenance of tourist and travel facilities and the establishment of accompanying services are important vehicles for economic growth and development, especially for those countries with natural tourism resources and limited industrial capability. Earnings from tourism and other *invisibles* (this term is explained later in the chapter) are particularly important for countries with deficits in merchandise trade.

This chapter explores the importance of international tourism as a commercial and economic activity and seeks to demonstrate the need for greater public policy awareness of tourism as an integral force in the economic development of the world and of the United States.

SERVICES EXPORT

The tourism export industry is a growing component of the services sector. Tradable business services represent a wealth of intangibles exported by U.S. firms—construction and engineering services, management consulting services, and many others—including all the food, lodging, transportation, and entertainment the U.S. provides to foreign visitors during their stay in the United States.

U.S. trade in business services has long been a positive factor in the overall U.S. current account performance and even more so since recent major improvements in collecting services data have been made.[5] The fact that improvements in collecting services data have been mandated by Congress and implemented by the executive branch and the fact that business services had a surplus of $19 billion in 1988 are causing a new look at the growing importance and recognition of services trade. Business services trade tends to be dominated by the large travel and transportation category (frequently referred to as the "tourism" sector of the economy).[6]

TRAVEL AND TRANSPORTATION

U.S. trade in travel and passenger fares has typically been in deficit, especially in periods marked by a strong dollar and strong growth in the U.S. economy (see Table 2.1). In every year since 1960, except in

TABLE 2.1

U.S. Business Services Trade, by Component, 1977–1988 (millions of dollars)

	Total Business Services			Travel			Passenger Fares		
	Exports	Imports	Balance	Exports	Imports	Balance	Exports	Imports	Balance
1977	23,374	20,866	2,508	6,150	7,451	−1,301	1,366	2,748	−1,382
1978	27,103	23,738	3,365	7,183	8,475	−1,292	1,603	2,896	−1,293
1979	31,155	27,157	3,998	8,441	9,413	−972	2,156	3,184	−1,028
1980	37,040	29,428	7,612	10,588	10,397	191	2,591	3,607	−1,016
1981	44,643	32,644	11,999	12,913	11,479	1,434	3,111	4,487	−1,376
1982	44,818	33,490	11,328	12,393	12,394	−1	3,174	4,772	−1,598
1983	45,300	36,361	8,939	10,947	13,149	−2,202	3,610	6,003	−2,393
1984	54,761	49,530	5,231	17,753	22,709	−4,956	4,015	5,910	−1,895
1985	56,942	53,569	3,373	17,937	24,517	−6,580	4,388	6,671	−2,283
1986	70,886	59,281	11,605	20,454	26,000	−5,546	5,546	6,774	−1,228
1987	79,405	67,455	11,950	23,505	29,215	−5,710	6,882	7,423	−541
1988	92,058	73,073	18,985	29,202	32,112	−2,910	8,860	7,872	988

	Shipping and Other Transp.			Royalties and License Fees			Other Business Services		
	Exports	Imports	Balance	Exports	Imports	Balance	Exports	Imports	Balance
1977	7,090	7,972	-882	4,920	505	4,415	3,848	2,190	1,658
1978	8,136	9,124	-988	5,885	670	5,215	4,296	2,573	1,723
1979	9,971	10,906	-935	6,184	831	5,353	4,403	2,822	1,581
1980	11,618	11,790	-172	7,085	724	6,361	5,158	2,909	2,249
1981	12,560	12,474	86	7,284	650	6,634	8,775	3,554	5,221
1982	12,317	11,710	607	5,177	617	4,560	11,757	3,997	7,760
1983	12,590	12,222	368	5,277	723	4,554	12,876	4,264	8,612
1984	13,809	14,843	-1,034	5,629	955	4,674	13,555	5,113	8,442
1985	14,674	15,643	-969	5,995	891	5,104	13,948	5,847	8,101
1986	15,458	16,715	-1,257	7,254	1,062	6,192	22,174	8,730	13,444
1987	16,989	18,062	-1,073	9,070	1,365	7,705	22,959	11,390	11,569
1988	18,930	19,641	-711	10,735	2,048	8,687	24,331	11,400	12,931

Note: Surplus [+], deficit [−].
Source: U.S. Department of Commerce, Bureau of Economic Analysis, *Survey of Current Business.*

1981 and 1989, the United States experienced combined travel and passenger-fare deficits. In 1988, the balance in travel and transportation improved considerably, and the overall deficit declined to $2.6 billion from $7.3 billion in 1987. Preliminary data for 1989 indicate that travel and passenger fares will be in surplus by about $1.2 billion, the first time since 1981 and the highest surplus ever in the account. Travel receipts (including passenger fares) gained from foreign tourists equaled $43.8 billion in 1989, which exceeded travel payments of $42.6 billion made by U.S. residents traveling abroad. The high value of the dollar in the early 1980s played a key role in enlarging this deficit. The strengthening dollar through early 1985 improved the price advantage of tourism services in many foreign countries, especially the major developed nations, but the decline in the dollar exchange rate thereafter did not result in major improvements in the combined travel and transportation balance until 1988.

Travel

The 24 percent growth in 1988 travel service exports—expenditures in the United States by foreign tourists and businesses—resulted in record receipts of $29.2 billion (see Table 2.1). Import growth (spending abroad by U.S. tourists and business travelers) of 10 percent resulted in record payments to foreigners of $32.1 billion. As a result, the U.S. travel deficit fell from $5.7 billion in 1987 to $2.9 billion in 1988.

Improvements in U.S. travel trade development, tourism policy initiatives, and the depreciation of the dollar since early 1985 have been significant factors in the growth of travel service exports since 1985. The dollar decline tended to lower costs for foreigners traveling in the United States and increased U.S. dollar costs for U.S. citizens traveling abroad. Nevertheless, not all travelers were so affected, as more than one third of U.S. international travel receipts and payments reflected transactions with Canada and Mexico—countries whose currencies have remained relatively stable in relation to the U.S. dollar.

Passenger Transportation

For the first time in recent history, the United States recorded a surplus in passenger transportation services in 1988 (see Table 2.1). The $1.0 billion surplus reversed the $0.5 billion deficit of 1987 and the record $2.4 billion deficit of 1983. U.S. passenger transportation exports—primarily fares paid by foreign residents to U.S. airlines—expanded very slowly during 1981–1985 but increased by about 25 percent annually over 1985–1988. The record 1988 receipts from transportation exports of $8.9 billion were almost double the 1985 total.

Passenger transportation imports—primarily fares paid by U.S. residents to foreign airlines—stagnated noticeably in 1986 after many years of consistent gains, increased by almost 10 percent in 1987, and increased by only 6 percent, to $7.9 billion, in 1988.

Two factors strongly affected the balance in this account: the number of U.S. versus foreign travelers, and whether they selected U.S. or non-U.S. carriers. The 1988 surplus appears to have reflected a substantial increase in the number of foreign residents using U.S. air carriers and increases in average fares.

COMPARATIVE ADVANTAGE

The United States is often perceived as having a comparative advantage in internationally traded private business services. The economic theory of comparative advantage in its basic interpretation simply states that countries will specialize in producing and exporting those goods and services in which they have an advantage in terms of land, labor, capital, technology, or other factors of production.[7] For example, a country that has petroleum, iron ore, agriculture soil, fishing waters, or similar resources would concentrate on the development, production, investment, and management of its resources to produce and export in those areas. The same is true for tourism. Good beaches, beautiful mountains, historic monuments, progressive transportation systems, and other attractions as potential tourism "products" are as important to a country as exports as are the production and export of more tangible products such as oil and steel. In fact, in some respects, tourism is a superior export product because much of the "productive capacity" is less exhaustible and causes less disruption and pollution of the environment.

The comparative advantage for tourism can often help developing nations earn foreign exchange more rapidly and with less difficulty than they could with other products. For example, it is interesting to note that international tourism in 1982 was proportionately more important for developing countries, accounting for about one third of their services trade, than it was for industrialized countries. It was the largest of four major services categories for the non-oil-exporting developing countries as a group. On the whole, industrialized countries had a deficit in the travel account, whereas developing countries had a surplus. Industrialized countries accounted for 70 to 75 percent of the travel.[8]

Probably no country in the world has a greater comparative advantage in tourism than the United States. It has an abundance of natural resources with tremendous tourism potential—such as magnificent mountains, wondrous valleys, beautiful beaches, lovely islands, spectacular forests, colorful deserts, impressive rolling plains, striking bodies of water (oceans, lakes, rivers, and streams), and immense isolated land masses. It has great cities and interesting small towns and villages. Other attractions abound, and there is a never-ending number of events, festivals, and local celebrations of interest to visitors. Participatory activities—swimming, scuba diving, sailing, surfing, boating, skiing (water and snow), camping, spelunking, hiking, hunting, bird watching, tennis, golf, and on and on—are limited only by the imagination. And there are a multiplicity of personal services and amenities that are particularly advantageous and conducive to business travel. In brief, the opportunities for participation in all aspects of tourism are greater in the United States than anywhere else in the world thus giving the United States a comparative advantage in tourism.

EMPLOYMENT

One of the reasons tourism is so important economically is that it is labor intensive. Tourism employment is concentrated mainly in the services sector rather than in the goods-producing sector, and the services sector tends to be less automated. Thus, much labor is used with relatively little capital. In the United States, tourism is one of the three largest employers in more than thirty states, generating about 6 million jobs and estimated payrolls totaling about $74 billion. Travel services directly generate more jobs than any other industry except health services.

The future of the U.S. economy will require many new jobs to absorb new workers into the labor force. The U.S. Department of Labor has predicted that, in the next decade, nine of every ten new jobs created will be in the service industries. Tourism offers an important source of those new jobs. The U.S. Department of Labor also predicts that by the end of this century, minorities, women, and immigrants will comprise 80 percent of the new entrants into the work force. Travel and tourism will play a key role in providing employment opportunities for these groups, which encounter the greatest difficulty in finding jobs. Tourism is a particularly good potential source of jobs because it is both labor intensive and likely to grow in the future, which means that for each additional dollar expended on the growing tourism sector, more jobs will be created than in most other areas of the economy.

While it demands large numbers of highly skilled workers and well-trained and educated managers, tourism has the further advantage of providing employment in the hard-to-employ, lower-skilled occupations. It is these occupations that have the highest unemployment rates and that are the most resistant to broad fiscal and monetary policy aimed at lower unemployment. For example, the travel industry in the United States provides a disproportionate number of jobs for the traditionally disadvantaged—blacks, Hispanic-Americans, and women. In 1987, this industry provided 970,000 jobs for blacks, (11.2 percent of total travel industry employment, compared to 10.1 percent nationally); 765,000 jobs for Hispanic-Americans (8.8 percent versus 6.9 percent nationwide); and nearly 4.6 million jobs for women (52.9 percent versus 44.8 percent of total U.S. employment).[9] Thus, "microeconomic" efforts concentrated on stimulating the growth of the tourist sector are more likely to create jobs for all levels and representative groups of the labor force than the "macroeconomic" measures of tax reduction, government expenditures, or increasing the rate of growth of the money supply.

INCOME

While creating jobs, international tourism is an important generator of national income as well. Foreign visitors make large expenditures in the United States—almost $44 billion in 1989—on a wide variety of goods and services, and these yield a substantial increase in income in the United States. For example, foreign travelers are interested in general sightseeing, good dining, cultural activities, and shopping for high-quality goods, which in turn represent a significant source of foreign exchange receipts.

In its broadest sense, tourism encompasses all expenditures for goods and services by travelers. It includes purchase of travelers checks, transportation, lodging, attractions, meals, beverages entertainment, souvenirs, car rentals, travel agency and sightseeing tour services, and personal grooming services. The full scope of international travel and tourism, therefore, covers the output of segments of many industries. In addition, tourist activities make use of the services of other industries, such as insurance, banking services, credit cards, auto clubs, park fees, taxi services, cameras and film, reservation systems, and telephones. One advantage of the foreign visitor over the domestic tourist is that international visitors spend almost six times as much on tourism services, and they add "fresh" rather than "recycled" dollars to the economy. But the overall impact on the U.S. economy is even greater than the actual expenditures for goods and services because of the tourism "multiplier."

MULTIPLIER EFFECT

An important point to bear in mind is that a nation's economic well-being is usually measured in terms of national income, which is the sum total of the flow of incomes from hand to hand. Economists have long realized that an increase in public or private investment in an economy increases national income by an amount greater than the amount invested. Economists use the term *multiplied amount* because, as it changes hands, the initial investment is re-spent and generates new rounds of spending.

MIT economist Paul Samuelson has pointed out that export earnings have the same "multiplier" effects on national income as an increase in domestic investment. International tourism receipts represent an infusion of fresh money from outside the economy and have the same impact as any other export in improving a nation's overall economy.

What economists also tell us, however, is that the multiplier is a double-edged sword. A sudden drop in investment, export earnings, or tourism receipts, reduces national income by a multiplied amount. A decline of $1 million in a nation's tourism earnings is therefore going to result in a decline of more than $1 million in that nation's national income. That decline will not only affect sales, profits, and employment in the tourism industry, it will also affect the fortunes of feeder industries that supply the tourism industry—agriculture, fishing, food processing and packing, floriculture, brewing and distilling, transportation, handicrafts, and many others.

An example of the multiplier effect is as follows: Monsieur A stays at the hotel of Ms. B one night and pays her $50. Ms. B uses part of the $50 to pay Ms. C, a hotel worker. Ms. C uses part of her wages to pay Mr. D, the butcher, who then buys bread from Ms. E, the baker, and the money originally spent by Monsieur A keeps moving through the economy generating a good deal more economic activity than the $50 he spent on the hotel room. There are varying estimates of the magnitude of the tourism multiplier, and it will vary from country to country and within a country as well. But it is likely to be between 2.0 and 4.0, meaning that a dollar expended on tourism in the U.S. will increase the U.S. gross national product by between $2 and $4.[10]

EXPORTING TOURISM

The tourism sector is highly diverse: part public, part private, and composed of many industries and many firms. It is estimated that more than one million enterprises are involved in travel-related businesses in the United States, of which 98 percent can be classified as small. These small firms include "mom and pop" travel agencies, family-owned motels, restaurants, amusement areas, and souvenir, gift, and other retail establishments. The tourism sector also includes large corporations that own hotel chains, airlines, cruiseship lines, bus lines, railroads, rental car agencies, theme parks, and airport catering operations. These individual firms collectively produce a travel product that is sometimes misrepresented and referred to as an "invisible" export. Yet, in terms of the balance of trade, tourism as a service export is equal to, for example, a "merchandise product." The *Dictionary of Economics* (by Harold S. Sloan and Arnold J. Zurcher, Barnes and Noble, Inc., New York, 1968) explains expenditures of tourists in a foreign country as follows: "Such expenditures are an invisible item of trade and have the same effect on the balance of payments of the tourists' home country as an import of merchandise from the country in which the expenditures are made" (p. 333).

Tourism is invisible in the sense that, as an export product, it is not produced, packaged, shipped, or received like "hard" goods. Consumers bring themselves to the point of sale, pay for the product (services) and, at some point in the future or almost immediately, receive the services. Furthermore, even though tourism may be sold abroad, it is consumed within the selling country, thus generating additional opportunities for selling other goods and services.

Another aspect of tourism that is contrary to the export of goods is the way it is marketed. For example, at an export trade show, most manufactured products will be available for display and to touch, whereas tourism is not sold by the product being there. It is sold by a respectable agent who represents the product through visual aids such as brochures, posters, slides, films, or videotapes.

The basic point is that while tourism, and some other service items, may have some special characteristics and so may not be as well understood in discussions of U.S. exports as, for example, merchandise items, such service activities, which generate foreign currencies, are important exports and impact on the trade balance.

ECONOMIC DEVELOPMENT

Tourism plays an important role in the economic and technological development of nations. It *a*. stimulates the development of basic infrastructure (such as airports, harbors, roads, sewers, and electrical power), *b*. contributes to the growth of domestic industries that supply the tourism industry (e.g., transportation, agriculture, food processing, commercial fishing, lumbering, construction), *c.* attracts foreign investment (especially in hotels), and *d.* facilitates the transfer of technology and technical know-how. Technology transfer has been particularly evident in the hotel industry, as hotels in developing countries have acquired computer-based reservations systems and have contracted with North American and Western European hotel corporations for management and manpower-development services. Many countries place strong emphasis on the demand and supply of tourism services as part of their overall economic development. On the demand side, it becomes necessary to first research the potential interests and motivations of tourists. Then, location and identification of the markets, marketing and promotion, and pricing techniques become the main elements of demand analysis. The supply of tourism services is less well understood.

Basic to the tourism product are several supply factors. Natural resources such as scenic land, good climatic conditions, flora, fauna, water, beaches, and so on, are basic to tourism development. The availability of water supply systems, sewage disposal plants, transportation facilities, and related kinds of infrastructure is fundamental to meeting the needs of tourists. Also needed are hotels, restaurants, shopping centers, taxis, planes, buses—an almost endless list of supply components that tourists have come to expect. Less easily defined are some of the "hospitality" services, such as friendliness of the host community, availability of the arts, entertainment, and other attributes and activities that enhance the tourist product and add value and quality.

A quality tourism product requires careful planning to ensure that the demand and supply components are equally available. If tourists like a tourism product, the receiving country can reap the benefits. But without a clear plan for tourism development, the economic benefits may be short-lived.

IMPACT ON LOCAL ECONOMY

Almost every local community in the world has some resource, attraction, activity, event, or special interest or adventure opportunity that can motivate a traveler. It may be a special fishing hole, a unique place for photographing or painting, a backpacking or horseback trail, a good location for ballooning, a white-water rafting river, some unusual festival, or a sporting event such as golf or tennis. The point is that there is hardly a place in rural or urban America (and most other countries as well) that is not conducive to tourism. Even if the community is not a destination in and of itself, it still may have tourism potential. It may be on a favorite route for travelers and thus sell gasoline, food, lodging, souvenirs, and services to visitors. Alternatively, it may not yet be an important travel destination, but may have the potential of developing into a tourist product.

Local benefits from tourism are usually in such categories as employment, income, diversification of economic base, tax revenues, visibility, and/or cultural benefits. Of particular importance to communities both large and small is the fact that small businesses dominate the travel and tourism industry. Of the 1.4 million travel-related business firms in the United States, 98 percent are classified as small businesses.[11] Whatever the case, tourism provides an economic opportunity for a local community to grow and diversify its economic base.

Rural Tourism in the United States

The problems of rural areas are well documented. Many have experienced population loss, especially among better-educated youth and skilled workers. Residents of rural communities lag behind in education. Across the country, the economic competitiveness of rural areas is declining, in part because rural communities depend upon too few sources of income.

Much of rural America is, and historically has been, poor. The Federal Government has provided record levels of price and income support to farmers over the last decade. Yet the "farm crisis" has now spread beyond the farm into businesses that traditionally have catered to the farmer.

Economic planners say that new industries must be developed to replace those that are dying and are no longer competitive, that undeveloped rural resources must be utilized, and that rural Americans must be taught new skills. They also point out that nonmetropolitan counties that depended on tourism, retirement income, and specialized government spending exhibited much greater stability during the "turbulent eighties" than those that were dependent on rural manufacturing, farming, coal mining, or oil drilling. Rural communities are seeing the need to seek economic development alternatives to the once-dominant industries of farming, ranching, and mining. Many look to their own attractiveness as potential for tourism development, often based upon the area's cultural, historic, ethnic, and geographic uniqueness. Such changes are increasingly being viewed as opportunities for keeping rural communities economically viable. The article "Revival Bought with Tourism Dollars," in *The New York Times,* January 10, 1990, states: "A small but growing number of American towns, no longer able to prosper from the industry, mining, or farming that once defined them, are using imagination and ingenuity in hopes of snaring some of the tourism dollars that usually flow to big metropolitan hot spots," and goes on to cite several examples.

Defined as all areas having less than 50,000 inhabitants, rural America contains about 25 percent of the U.S. population and 90 percent of its natural resources.[12] Rural environments have vast expanses of land and water and wide diverse topographies (mountains, plains, forests, grasslands, and deserts) that provide outstanding settings for tourism and recreation.

At the specific direction of the U.S. Congress, tourism as an economic development tool for rural areas was studied extensively in 1989. As part of the 1988 budget process, Congress directed that the U.S. Department of Commerce's tourism agency, the United States Travel and Tourism Administration (USTTA), undertake a two-part national study to determine:

- the ways in which small business in rural areas can be promoted through travel and tourism; and

- whether there is a need for federal policy concerning the development and promotion of small businesses in rural communities through travel and tourism, and whether or not there should be a federal program to support such a policy.

To carry out this mandate, USTTA, through a contractor (Economics Research Associates), prepared *The National Policy Study on Rural Tourism and Small Businesses* in September 1989.[13] A companion part of this study was a special *Report of the Federal Task Force on Rural Tourism to the Tourism Policy Council* (September 25, 1989). This important research clearly demonstrated the positive potential that tourism possesses as an economic development tool for rural America and the need for a federal policy for rural tourism. These two research studies were supplemented by a special research report, *Enterprise Zones and Rural Tourism Development: Policy Issues and Options,* prepared by Hannah R. Messerli at the request of USTTA for the Committee on Rural Tourism Development of the Tourism Policy Council.

In January 1990, the Economic Policy Council Working Group on Rural Development issued the report, *Rural Economic Development for the 90's: A Presidential Initiative,* which included several references to tourism. It stated: "Any new lifeblood for rural America will be found primarily in off-farm employment opportunities, especially in industries such as tourism, retirement living, and commercial recreation, which all bring additional income to rural communities." In the 1990s, Congress will likely consider legislation that includes rural tourism.

ECONOMICS OF TOURISM INFORMATION

It is generally accepted in the business world that "information" gener-ates "power." And in today's world, through our various com-munications networks and new technology, information can be "beamed," "faxed," "telephoned," "cabled," or transmitted by tourists almost instantaneously. One means for such transmission of informa-tion in the business world is "teleconferencing." Teleconferencing is defined as "communication between people or groups of people at a distance from each other, an electronic device or medium being used to link them."[14] The implication of teleconferencing for travel and tour-ism, particularly with respect to business travel, could change aspects of business travel. Teleconferencing is just one small part of the de-velopment of "information technology." Another aspect of this technol-ogy is "interactive videotext or viewdata." A television screen is used to display information from an electronic information and message-sending system. Again, the potential uses for such a system for transmitting travel information are limited only by one's imagina-tion.[15]

As important as the information flows by electronic means are the informal communications systems of human beings traveling from one place to another. This informal human information "system" which is a part of the "information economy" is of great economic and social value. While the value of information transmitted through travel has not been quantified, it offers an important potential channel to further increase worldwide understanding.[16]

NOTES

1. An excellent compilation and analysis of the facts and figures regarding world travel is contained in *Travel Industry World Yearbook—The Big Picture*, by Somerset R. Waters, published by Child and Waters Inc., 1990. A more detailed discussion of the formulation of tourism policy as an aid in the overall planning and management of tourism can be found in Chapter 3: "The Formulation of Tourism Policy—A Managerial Framework" (Edgell, 1987), in the book *Travel, Tourism, and Hospital-ity Research*, edited by J. R. Brent Ritchie and Charles R. Goeldner and published by John Wiley and Sons (1987). Also see "Role of Tourism in the International Economic Policy of the United States," as presented by David L. Edgell and Stephen A. Wandner at the Western Economic Association Annual Meeting at Honolulu on June 22, 1978.

2. Estimates by author based on information provided for the most part by the World Tourism Organization, but from other sources as well.

3. *Charting a Course for International Tourism in the Nineties,* U.S. Department of Commerce, Washington, D.C., February 1990, p. 10.

4. *U.S. Industrial Outlook 1990,* "Travel Service." U.S. Department of Commerce, February 1990.

5. A special Benchmark Survey on services trade during 1986 was conducted by the Bureau of Economic Analysis (BEA), U.S. Department of Commerce. Results of this survey were published in the October 1988 *Survey of Current Business.* The survey was conducted pursuant to the amended provisions of the International Investment and Trade in Services Survey Act. BEA experts plan to update this data annually using sample surveys. The "travel" portion of trade data in business services has also been improved. The BEA now uses the data contained in the *Inflight Survey* produced by the U.S. Travel and Tourism Administration, U.S. Department of Commerce, for the travel statistics. Recent improvements and changes in the travel data are described in *Business America,* July 17, 1989.

6. An excellent treatment on the subject of services exports can be found in the publication *Services Exports—A Critical Force in International Trade,* Travel and Tourism Government Affairs Council, 1985. See also "U.S. Business Services Trade," in *United States Trade Performance,* U.S. Department of Commerce, Washington, D.C., September 1989, pp. 39–44 and p. 89. This publication defines business services, including travel and tourism, and details the importance of services trade as a part of the overall U.S. trade account; it is the source of most of the information in this section.

7. See Note 2 in Chapter 1.

8. See pp. 257–58 of the *U.S. National Study on Trade in Services,* Government Printing Office, Washington, D.C., December 1983.

9. *The United States Travel Industry,* United States Travel and Tourism, 1990.

10. See Note 5 in Chapter 1.

11. *Tourism USA* (Guidelines for Tourism Development). Prepared by the University of Missouri for the U.S. Department of Commerce, Washington, D.C., (revised and expanded 1986), pp. 1–2.

12. Charting a Course for International Tourism in the Nineties, U.S. Department of Commerce, February 1990, p. 19.

13. This *Study* is comprehensive and includes six appendices. It gives a very clear and comprehensive analysis of rural tourism. The *Study* was prepared for the United States Travel and Tourism Administration by Economics Research Associates in association with The University of Missouri and the United States Travel Data Center, Washington, D.C., September 1989.

14. See "Teleconferencing and its Effects on Business Travel," by Carole S. Fein, in *Tourism Management,* December 1983, p. 279.

15. See "Information Technology: Changes in the Travel Trade," by Margaret Bruce, in *Tourism Management,* December 1983, pp. 290–95.

16. An excellent presentation of the broad ramifications of travel and the information economy is contained in *The Role of Travel in the Information Economy,* by Cord D. Hansen-Sturm, January 1985.

An interesting commentary on the use of tourism as an economic development tool is presented in "Revival Bought with Tourist Dollars," *The New York Times,* January 10, 1990.

SUPPLEMENTAL READINGS

Destination USA. Report of the National Tourism Resources Review Commission, U.S. Government Printing Office, Washington, D.C., June 1973.

The Dictionary of Hospitality, Travel and Tourism (3rd Edition). Charles J. Metelka. Albany, New York: Delmar Publishers, Inc., 1990.

The Economic and Social Importance of International Tourism on Developing Countries. Robert Cleverdon. The Economist Intelligence Unit Special Report No. 60, May 1979.

"Economic Impact of Rural Festivals and Special Events: Assessing the Distribution of Expenditures." P. Long and R. Perdue. *Journal of Travel Research* (1989).

"International Tourism and Economic Development: A Special Case for Latin America." M. E. Bond and Jerry R. Ladman. In *Mississippi: Valley Journal of Business and Economics,* New Orleans, Vol. VIII, Fall 1972, No. 1, pp. 43–55.

National Policy Study on Rural Tourism and Small Business Development. Prepared for the United States Travel and Tourism Administration by Economics Research Associates. Vienna, Virginia: Economics Research Associates, September 1989.

"Recreation Development in Rural Communities: A Planning Process." P. Long, L. Perdue, and S. Kieselbach. *Journal of the American Planning Association* (1988).

Report of the Federal Task Force on Rural Tourism to the Tourism Policy Council. U.S. Department of Commerce, United States Travel and Tourism Administration, Washington, D. C., September 25, 1989.

"Revival Bought with Tourist Dollars." *The New York Times,* January 10, 1990.

Rural Economic Development for the 90's: A Presidential Initiative. The findings and recommendations of the Economic Policy Council Working Group on Rural Development as issued by Secretary of Agriculture Clayton Yeutter, January 1990.

"Rural Resident Attitudes and Perceptions." R. Perdue, P. Long, and L. Allen. Symposium on Leisure Research, National Recreation and Park Association Annual Congress, San Antonio, Texas (1989).

Rural Tourism in Europe. Council of Europe, Publications and Documents Division, Strasbourg 1988.

Tourism—Past, Present and Future. A. J. Burkart and S. Medlick. New York: International Publications Service, 1975.

Tourism Statistical Information in Relation to Policy Decision Making. David L. Edgell and Stephen A. Wandner. Paper presented at the Joint National Meeting of the Operations Research Society–The Institute of Management Sciences, Atlanta, November 9, 1977.

The Travel Industry (2nd Edition). Chuck Y. Gee, James C. Makens, and Dexter J. L. Choy. New York: Van Nostrand Reinhold, 1989.

Travel Industry World Yearbook—The Big Picture, 1989. Somerset R. Waters. New York: Child and Waters, 1989.

Turismo En Espacio Rural. Venancio Bote Gomez. Madrid: Editorial Popular, S. A., 1989.

"World Prospects for Tourism (Part One)." David L. Edgell. *World Travel*, No. 137, August–September 1979, pp. 33–38.

"World Prospects for Tourism (Part Two)." David L. Edgell. *World Travel*, No. 138, October–November 1977, pp. 38–40.

CHAPTER 3

POLITICAL AND FOREIGN POLICY IMPLICATIONS OF INTERNATIONAL TOURISM

Tourism is a simple continuation of politics by other means.

Jean-Maurice Thurot, Economia, May 1975.

THE POLITICAL ECONOMY OF TOURISM

The political aspects of tourism are interwoven with its economic consequences. Thus, tourism is not only a "continuation of politics" but an integral part of the world's political economy. In short, tourism is, or can be, a tool used not only for economic but for political means. For obvious economic reasons, most countries seek to generate a large volume of inbound tourism. As we learned in Chapter 2, expenditures by foreign visitors add to national income and employment and are a valuable source of foreign exchange earnings. Various measures are taken by governments to encourage foreigners to visit their respective territories. Promotion offices are established in key countries, bolstered by extensive advertising campaigns to attract tourists. Today more than 170 governments maintain travel-promotion offices around the world. Most are located in the principal travel-generating countries of Western Europe, the United States, Canada, Mexico, and Japan. Visas are issued freely for temporary visitors, and other entry requirements are held to a minimum to avoid discouraging potential tourists (the United States is more restrictive than Western Europe, Canada, Mexico, and Japan in its entry procedures). At home, governments seek to stimulate the construction of needed tourist infrastructure, access roads, communications, airport facilities, and the many other supply-side requirements for supporting tourism. Efforts are devoted to conserving areas of natural beauty and developing and maintaining resort areas and sightseeing attractions. Special events, entertainment, and cultural activities are often encouraged by local and national governments. Other services performed by governments, such as police protection and crime control and maintaining good health and sanitary conditions, are also necessary to support tourism.

Tourism Facilitation

A number of political, economic, and social factors influence the government actions and regulations that affect tourism. Travel bans are imposed from time to time for political reasons. It is not unusual, for example, for governments to prohibit travel of their citizens to war zones or to territories of hostile nations, where the government has no means of protecting the life and property of the citizens. The U.S. State Department, for instance, through its Citizens Emergency Center, issues travel advisories to warn Americans considering going abroad about adverse conditions they might find in specific countries.[1] Special precautions also may be taken when outbreaks of contagious diseases occur in foreign countries. These measures may result in discouraging or inconveniencing tourists. Also, some burdensome practices (exhaustive inspections of luggage, body searches) may be instituted for passenger safety and security and to prevent smuggling.

Another concern of governments is immigration control. Nearly all countries strictly control the entrance of immigrants and enforce laws against illegal entrants. Of particular concern are the social pressures created by the need to care for jobless immigrants and the opposition of the local labor force when jobs are scarce.

To even admit foreign visitors and to facilitate their travel within a nation's borders is a political action. Therefore, the way in which a nation's international tourism is approached becomes an aspect of its foreign policy, as well as a part of its economic and commercial policy.[2]

Examples of the political and foreign policy implications of international tourism are endless. The history of travel contains numerous references to international tourism with political overtones, ranging from Marco Polo's vivid descriptions of the political events in the orient to the uncertainty, lack of knowledge, and myths associated with the "dark continent" of Africa prior to its exploration by the Europeans. Following are examples to illustrate the broad policy implications of international tourism in today's world.

Increased contacts between persons of different cultures can lead to increased knowledge and understanding, which, in turn, can contribute to a relaxation of tensions between nations. For example, the Shanghai Communiqué, signed in 1972 by the United States and the People's Republic of China, noted in part that "the effort to reduce tensions is served by improving communications between countries that have different ideologies, so as to lessen the risks of confrontation through accident, miscalculation or misunderstanding."[3]

There are numerous additional examples, but none more dramatic than what occurred in 1989 in Eastern Europe. Few individuals could have predicted the demise of the Berlin Wall in 1989 or the graphic television pictorials of soldiers cutting down the "Iron Curtain." Such changes are having profound effects upon East—West travel and will continue to do so through the 1990s. The result will be a deeper understanding among peoples of the world, increased commerce, and a greater step toward international cooperation. It will be some time before we know just what the political implications of such human contact will be.

Even in a country like Cuba, where tourism is sometimes referred to as a "bourgeois" custom, international tourism is returning after a thirty-year hiatus. In "Reviving the Allure of Cuba," an article dated August 3, 1987, in *The Washington Post,* it was pointed out that in Cuba's effort to earn hard currency it is now encouraging foreign visitors.[4] By 1985, Cuba saw 173,000 foreign visitors, mostly from Canada and Western Europe. According to "In Search of Tourists" in *Newsweek,* December 19, 1988, the number of foreign tourists grew to 211,464 by 1987.[5] In a companion *Newsweek* article, "White Sand, Blue Seas and Big Dreams" (January 9, 1989), the tourism conflict for Cuba was cited as the need to dramatically increase tourism without upsetting "the socialist life it is trying to build for its own citizens." Whatever the case, as more tourists visit Cuba, there will be political impacts of one kind or another.[6]

Tourism and Foreign Policy

The prospective economic benefits of tourism frequently influence the internal policies of governments. In some corners of our globe, inbound tourism is used to showcase the accomplishments of the government or party in power and to increase understanding abroad of the government's policies. Sometimes this approach is successful, sometimes it backfires. The point is that tourism expands the horizon of the tourist and presents the host government or community with a unique opportunity to influence visitors from abroad, and vice versa. Alternatively, countries, including the United States, sponsor numerous exchanges, cultural programs, lecture series, and other events to make people of the world aware of country customs and standards of living. At the same time, a country must be made safe for tourism. Civil strife and disorders, such as those that have wracked Northern Ireland and Lebanon, have a detrimental impact on tourism. In addition, the wave of terrorism in the mid 1980s weighed heavily on international tourism.

According to Jean-Maurice Thurot, tourists create an economic dependence by the host country on tourist-generating countries. This dependence can influence the foreign policy of the host country toward the generating country. This is especially true in nations needing foreign exchange, or hard currency, for economic development. Nations in the process of economic development need to buy key items, especially capital equipment and technology, from the industrial nations in order to speed their own growth. International tourism can be an engine of economic growth by providing an important source of foreign exchange. Most socialist countries and less-developed nations need tourist revenues, especially hard Western currencies, for economic growth. Government policy changes can accommodate tourism and thus decrease the need for merchandise exports.

Agreements Beyond Just Tourism

Tourism has become embedded in treaties and trade agreements designed and negotiated largely for other reasons. The most well-known international agreement containing tourism provisions is the human rights section of the 1975 *Helsinki Accord,* which was the *Final Act of the Conference on Security and Cooperation in Europe.* The better-known section of this Accord deals with the rights of people to migrate freely, but in the tourism sections the thirty-five nations—including the United States and the Soviet Union—acknowledged that freer tourism is essential to the development of cooperation amongst nations. With specific reference to tourism, the signatories to the Accord, among other points, *a.* expressed their intentions to "encourage increased tourism on both an individual and group basis," *b.* recognized the desirability of carrying out "detailed studies on tourism," *c.* agreed to "endeavor, where possible, to ensure that the development of tourism does not injure the artistic, historic and cultural heritage in their respective countries," *d.* stated their intention "to facilitate wider travel by their citizens for personal or professional reasons," *e.* agreed to "endeavor gradually to lower, where necessary, the fees for visas and official travel documents," *f.* agreed to "increase, on the basis of appropriate agreements or arrangements, cooperation in the development of tourism, in particular, by considering bilaterally, possible ways to increase information relating to travel to other related questions of mutual interest," and *g.* expressed their intention "to promote visits to their respective countries."[7]

But the hopes of this Conference and the potential of tourism as an agent of political reapproachment will be realized only through the efforts of governments, national tourist offices, and private industry. The record, until recently, has not been a promising one.

Tourism as a foreign policy tool was exercised in part by the U.S. Government in 1980, after the Soviet invasion of Afghanistan, when President Carter encouraged Americans and the U.S. Olympic Committee to boycott the 1980 Moscow Olympic Games. There was more than a 75-percent drop in American travel to the Soviet Union during the year. Tour operators abandoned travel to the Soviet Union and Eastern European markets in 1980–1981. There was a decided shift in tourism patterns. A somewhat similar situation occurred in 1984, when the East Bloc countries, spurred on by the Soviets (and with the exception of Romania), boycotted the Olympic Games in Los Angeles. Hoping to avoid future such happenings, the United States and the Soviet Union on September 15, 1985, signed an "Accord of Mutual Understanding and Cooperation in Sports," which is a step toward future cooperation in the Olympic Games. There are many other examples where sports—tourism programs have served as powerful public diplomacy tools and bridges for international understanding, even when the political climate between countries is not agreeable.

Since 1985, the United States and the Soviet Union have made steady progress in establishing closer ties through tourism. In Geneva in 1985, the two governments signed a *General Agreement on Contacts and Exchanges*. Article XIV of this agreement commits both sides to promote tourism as a vehicle for broader familarization of each other's peoples, life, work, and culture. This was followed by the resumption of direct air service between the Soviet Union and the United States in April 1986. In November 1989, Pan American, Aeroflot, and Sheraton Hotels entered into a trilateral arrangement to foster the development of an international hotel in Moscow. Furthermore, on May 29, 1990, during a Washington, D.C., press ceremony, the Radisson Hotels International (headquartered in Minneapolis, Minnesota) unveiled their plans to open an American Business Center later this year in Moscow. This hotel, which will be the first American-managed hotel and business complex in the Soviet Union, will feature hi-tech accoutrements as well as 430 rooms and 165 suites. And finally, on June 1, 1990, during the summit meetings between President George Bush and General Secretary Mikhail Gorbachev, a side letter on tourism matters was signed as part of the U.S.–U.S.S.R. Agreement on Trade Relations.

The Soviet Union has long recognized the political and foreign policy value of tourism. The resolution of the 27th Congress of the Communist Party of the Soviet Union, held in 1986, and the "Guidelines for the Economic and Social Development of the Soviet Union for 1986–1990 and for the Period Ending in 2000" contain numerous provisions directly connected with developing international trade in tourism relations between the Soviet Union and other countries of the world.[8]

INTERNATIONAL TOURISM POLICY FOR THE UNITED STATES

Similarly, the United States, through the National Tourism Policy Act of 1981 (see Appendix B), has put more emphasis on broader policy goals, which often impact on, or are related to, foreign policy goals. For example, under Title I of this Act, two of the twelve national tourism policy goals are to "contribute to personal growth, health, education, and intercultural appreciation of the geography, history, and ethnicity of the United States" and to "encourage the free and welcome entry of individuals traveling to the United States, in order to enhance international understanding and goodwill. . . ." Furthermore, Title II of the Act states that USTTA "should consult with foreign governments on travel and tourism matters and, in accordance with applicable law, represent United States travel and tourism interests before international and intergovernmental meetings. . . ." This latter provision of the Act gives USTTA the authority to meet, negotiate, and discuss a broad range of international tourism trade issues either bilaterally or multilaterally.

The National Tourism Policy Act of 1981, 22 U.S.C section 2121 *et seq.,* in addition to the above, also directs the Secretary of Commerce to administer a comprehensive program to encourage travel to the United States, reduce barriers to travel, and generally facilitate international travel. Section 2123 authorizes the Secretary, *inter alia,* to consult with foreign governments on travel and tourism matters, establish branches of official tourism offices in foreign countries, and assist in training and education on travel and tourism matters. The Act provides that the duties of the Secretary of Commerce in its administration may be exercised by the Under Secretary of Commerce for Travel and Tourism. The Under Secretary heads the U.S. Travel and Tourism Administration.[9]

On a limited scale, the United States Travel and Tourism Administration (USTTA) has fostered international tourism policies through international representations and bilateral negotiations with other countries. USTTA, in concert with the U.S. Department of State and other affected agencies, has negotiated tourism agreements with several countries. Fundamentally, tourism agreements are diplomatic arrangements prescribing reciprocal measures to reduce travel restrictions, facilitate two-way trade in tourism, and establish the status of the parties' official travel promotion offices. However, each and every agreement has different and separate provisions, depending upon the circumstances and concerns of the two countries. Most include the exchange of information and statistics as well as promoting greater understanding and goodwill through international tourism.

TOURISM AGREEMENTS

Since 1978, the United States has negotiated tourism agreements with eight countries: Mexico, Venezuela, Egypt, the Philippines, Hungary, Yugoslavia, Poland, and Morocco. The most comprehensive agreements are with Mexico and Venezuela, both negotiated and signed in 1989 (see Appendices C and D). The first consultation and implementation of the U.S.–Mexico Tourism Agreement took place in Mexico City on November 21, 1989 (see Appendix E). While the concept behind a tourism agreement is the promotion of trade in tourism, these bilateral agreements also serve additional national policy objectives, such as encouraging international understanding, friendly relations, and goodwill. Basically the tourism agreements entered into by the U.S. government:

- aim to increase two-way tourism

- support efforts by the National Tourism Organization travel-promotion office(s)

- improve tourism facilitation

- encourage investments in each other's tourism industry

- promote the sharing of research, statistics, and information

- recognize the importance of the safety and security of tourists

- suggest mutual cooperation on policy issues in international tourism

- provide for regular consultations on tourism matters

- acknowledge benefits from education and training in tourism

- enhance mutual understanding and goodwill

These two agreements with Mexico and Venezuela differ from some other agreements on tourism by providing that each party, on a reciprocal basis, will accredit tourism-promotion personnel of the other party as members of a diplomatic mission or consular post. This is in accordance with a movement by many countries (including the United States) to recognize that tourism activities of a national tourism office constitute a legitimate diplomatic and consular function within the meaning of Article 3 of the Vienna Convention of Diplomatic Relations. Such recognition gives stature to international tourism promotion and puts it on a more equal footing with other governmental activities.

The United States and Canada signed a Free Trade Agreement (FTA) on January 2, 1988, which took effect on January 1, 1989, and which includes a tourism Annex (see Appendix F). Under the FTA, the United States and Canada will accord "national treatment" to tourism services. National treatment means treatment no less favorable than the most favorable treatment accorded by a province or state to those residing within that province or state.[10] The FTA also specifies that annual consultations take place regarding the implementation of the tourism Annex of the FTA. The first such consultation took place the week of November 30, 1989, in Washington, D.C. The results of the consultation on tourism (consultations on other sectors were also taking place) were summarized in a "Report by the Working Group on Tourism," issued in Washington D.C. on November 30, 1989 (see Appendix G).

INTERGOVERNMENTAL ORGANIZATIONS

There are at least eight intergovernmental organizations identified as being involved with international policy relating to problems and issues in tourism.[11] Three principal organizations are the Organization of American States (OAS), the Organization for Economic Cooperation and Development (OECD), and the World Tourism Organization (WTO). Following is a very brief description of the involvement of these organizations with international tourism. In Chapter 4, some additional remarks will be made regarding the impact of intergovernmental organization treatment of barriers to international tourism.

Organization of American States (OAS)

The OAS, headquartered in Washington, D.C., is currently composed of the following countries: Antigua and Barbuda, Argentina, the Bahamas, Barbados, Bolivia, Brazil, Canada, Chile, Colombia, Costa Rica, Cuba, Dominica, Dominican Republic, Ecuador, El Salvador, Grenada, Guatemala, Haiti, Honduras, Jamaica, Mexico, Nicaragua, Panama, Paraguay, Peru, St. Kitts and Nevis, Saint Lucia, Saint Vincent and the Grenadines, Surinam, Trinidad and Tobago, the United States, Uruguay, and Venezuela. The most important tourism meeting in which all of the OAS countries participate is the Inter-American Travel Congress.

The OAS held its first Inter-American Travel Congress (which meets every three years) in San Francisco in 1939. Much of the significant work of the OAS in tourism was accomplished through its Tourism Development Program, formed in 1970. The main functions were to assist member tourism authorities in developing and promoting their respective tourism sectors; to support member states' efforts to create appropriate conditions for increasing the flow of tourism to the region; to provide broad policy advice on tourism issues; and to coordinate with international bodies on tourism matters. The principal policy bodies of the OAS tourism program are the Executive Committee (seven elected member nations which meet about once a year) and the Inter-American Travel Congress (which meets every three years and also includes invited observers from nations that are not members). Some of the important tourism matters dealt with have included financing mechanisms, facilitation, statistics, and education and training. In a recent reorganization of the OAS, the tourism programs have been integrated into the OAS Department of Regional Development.

Over the years, the OAS has viewed tourism as having broad policy implications beyond the narrow economic benefits so important to most of the countries. At a "special" meeting of the Inter-American Travel Congress in Rio de Janeiro, Brazil, on August 25, 1972, the OAS formulated the *Declaration of Rio de Janeiro* (see Appendix H), an important document that relates tourism to some of the broader issues. This document was reinforced through the *Declaration of Caracas* at the XIII Inter-American Travel Congress, Caracas, Venezuela, September 24, 1977. In addition, the OAS has been an effective partner in the numerous activities underway to celebrate the Christopher Columbus Quincentennial Jubilee regarding the arrival of Christopher Columbus in the Western Hemisphere in 1492. The planning for this event is taking place under the auspices of the "Quincentennial Commemoration of the Discovery of America: The Encounter of Two Worlds, and Opportunities for Tourism Promotion."

Organization for Economic Cooperation and Development (OECD)

The OECD, headquartered in Paris, is a forum for consultations and discussions by most of the industrialized countries of the world on a broad range of economic issues. The OECD countries are: Austria, Belgium, Denmark, Finland, France, Germany, Greece, Iceland, Ireland, Italy, Luxembourg, the Netherlands, Norway, Portugal, Spain, Sweden, Switzerland, Turkey, the United Kingdom, Canada, the United States, Australia, New Zealand, and Japan. Through various committees and working groups, the OECD conducts studies and negotiations to solve trade and related problems and to coordinate its policies for purposes of other international negotiations. The OECD Tourism Committee reviews problems in international travel and tourism among member countries and publishes statistics and policy changes in a yearly report, *Tourism Policy and International Tourism in OECD Member Countries.*

For over twenty-five years the Tourism Committee has published this annual report, which describes the main features of what have come to be called the national tourism policies of the OECD member countries and Yugoslavia. While Yugoslavia is not an official OECD member, it is an invited observer to all OECD activities. For the past few years, the report has set out the aims and priorities of each country's tourism policy and listed the most important tourism policy measures adopted in the previous year, thereby making it possible to keep abreast of policy developments in each member country.

The Committee also considers that it is necessary to examine the national tourism policies of member countries as a whole, so as to show their broad trends. Its role is not only to permit an exchange of information on tourism policies, but also to promote a consensus on the choice and direction of policies compatible with the OECD's aims. This presupposes an overall view and better understanding of the past, present, and future concerns of the tourism authorities' policies.

In 1982, the OECD member countries turned their attention to barriers to travel. A list of obstacles to travel was compiled in 1983, and the OECD began to deliberate on ways to reduce those impediments. A milestone was achieved in November 1985, when the OECD Council adopted a new instrument on international tourism policy that set forth principles aimed toward facilitating tourism for the twenty-four member countries. This is a major attempt at reducing restrictions on tourism and setting in motion a process of liberalization. By 1987, the member countries agreed to a new policy to liberalize foreign exchange allowances. This led to greater emphasis by national tourism policymakers in the OECD member countries to begin placing more emphasis on the quality side of tourism. This interest will likely continue into the 1990s.[12]

World Tourism Organization (WTO)

The only worldwide (109 member countries in 1989) tourism organization is the WTO, headquartered in Madrid. Formally established on January 2, 1975, it provides a world clearinghouse for the collection, analysis, and dissemination of technical tourism information. It offers national tourism administrations and organizations the machinery for a multinational approach to international discussions and negotiations on tourism matters. It includes more than 150 affiliate members (important private sector companies) interested in international dialogue and implementation of worldwide conferences, seminars, and other means for focusing on important tourism development issues and policies. WTO is also an implementing agency on technical assistance in tourism for the United Nations Development Program. WTO has an important Facilitation Committee whose aims are to propose measures to simplify entry and exit formalities, report on existing governmental requirements or practices that may impede the development of international travel, and develop a set of standards and recommended practices for a draft convention to facilitate travel and tourist stays through passport, visa and health, and exchange control measures. WTO also has a classification of travelers (see Figure 3.1).

The WTO has conveyed its broad concerns for all aspects of tourism through a number of special documents. The most popular and most often cited document is the *Manila Declaration on World Tourism*, prepared during the World Tourism Conference held at Manila, the Philippines, from September 27 to October 10, 1980, as sponsored by the WTO (see Appendix I). Another important document is the *Tourism Bill of Rights and Tourist Code* (see Appendix J). After several years of consultations and negotiations, the *Tourism Bill of Rights and Tourist Code* was adopted by the Sixth General Assembly of WTO in Sofia, Bulgaria, in September 1985 (more about this document in Chapter 5). The most recent document of note is *The Hague Declaration on Tourism* (see Appendix K). *The Hague Declaration on Tourism* was adopted during the InterParliamentary Conference on Tourism, April 10–14, 1989, jointly sponsored by the Inter-Parliamentary Union and the WTO.

While considerable progress has been made in utilizing tourism as an international policy tool for greater economic development and improved communication, cooperation, mutual understanding, and goodwill, much remains to be accomplished. Barriers to international tourism continue to exist and in some circumstances have increased. (This topic is discussed in detail in Chapter 4.) And while it may be overly optimistic to expect that the WTO's motto, "Tourism: passport to peace," will be shared by everyone, it is a step in the right direction. We do know that when peace prevails, tourism flourishes.[13]

INTERNATIONAL TERRORISM

A discussion of the political and foreign policy implications of international tourism would not be complete in today's world without mention of international terrorism and its impact on tourism.[14] Terrorism is not new; it is an age-old economic weapon. The history books are full of accounts of terrorism, hostage-taking, and kidnappings. The infamous period of piracy on the high seas with its plunder and

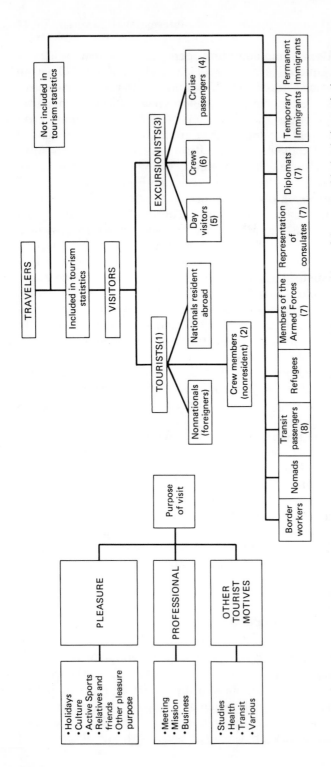

1. Visitors who spend at least one night in the country visited.
2. Foreign air or ship crews docked or in lay over and who use the accomodation establishments of the country visited.
3. Visitors who do not spend the night in the country visited although they may visit the country during one or more days and return to their ship or train to sleep.
4. Normally included in excursionists. Separate classification of these visitors is nevertheless recommended.
5. Visitors who come and leave the same day.
6. Crew who are not residents of the country visited and who stay in the country for the day.
7. When they travel from their country of origin to the duty station and vice-versa (including household servants and dependents accompanying or joining them).
8. Who do not leave the transit area of the airport or the port. In certain countries, transit may involve a stay of one or more days. In this case, they should be included in the visitors statistics.

Figure 3.1. Classification of travelers. (Source: World Tourism Organization)

violence was a time of terrorism and kidnapping which wrought havoc on the maritime industry.

What is new in terrorism is its use to attain political ends and the global attention that media coverage of terrorist incidents focuses on political causes. Also new are some of the responses; for example, the U.S. attack on Libya and various countries' use of military personnel to assault hijackers while a plane is on the ground. The horror of these events and their highly publicized results were enough to cause many travelers to reconsider their vacation plans. In a December 28, 1986, article in *The Washington Post*, "U.S. Travel Industry Has 'Worst Year Ever'," (which actually refers to the downturn in travel to Europe), it is mentioned that international terrorism, the Chernobyl nuclear accident in the Soviet Union (and concern of the possible spread of radiation fallout across Europe), the decline of the U.S. dollar, and the relatively inexpensive price of gas in the United States combined to cause Americans to travel domestically and not internationally in 1986. The article pointed out that the twenty-three Western European Nations took the brunt of the economic effects, with tourism in June 1986 down 41 percent from the same month in 1985.

One of the terrorists' principal objectives is to exact a price, to inflict an economic penalty, to punish governments for public policies and political behavior; in short, to make it prohibitively expensive for a government to carry out policies terrorists find unacceptable. By murdering innocent tourists, blowing up airliners and airline ticket offices, bombing airport terminals and railroad tunnels, and hijacking airliners, buses, and cruise ships, terrorists seek to

- frighten away tourists

- deny governments and populations the commercial and economic benefits of tourism

- force governments to rethink and abandon specific policies

The response by governments and the private sector to the impact of terrorism in tourism surpasses any prior attentions to security. The U.S. Federal Aviation Administration has increased its inspections of airports worldwide. Airport authorities have increased security systems within the airports. Private sector groups have conducted training sessions to deal with potential terrorism. Such efforts help, but for many pleasure travelers the worry, strain, and inconvenience are not worth it. They simply choose alternative destinations. It will take a strong concerted effort of global cooperation if the terrorism of the 1980s is to be avoided in the 1990s.

NOTES

1. A good explanation of travel advisories is contained in *Tour and Travel News,* June 5, 1989.

2. See Note 5 in Chapter 1, pp. 171–177.

3. Shanghai Communiqué (February 27, 1972). A joint statement issued at the conclusion of President Richard M. Nixon's visit to China.

4. This article also contains an interesting commentary on various paradoxes facing Cuba—the country is developing tourism for foreigners but doesn't want ordinary Cubans mixing with the tourists.

5. The article suggests that tourism may replace sugar as Cuba's main source of hard currency. As tourism increases, there is a greater need for new infrastructure, and Cuba is now seeking joint venture arrangements with foreign companies (mostly with Spain so far).

6. Tourism is already causing changes that somehow seem to clash with Cuba's ideologies. For example, the article cited mentions that Ernest Hemingway, an American, is frequently used as a promotional gimmick to attract tourism. There are presumably all kinds of "re-created" bars and restaurants advertising that Hemingway had been there or that it was his favorite place.

7. The Conference on Security and Cooperation in Europe, Final Act (commonly referred to as the Helsinki Accord) was signed by thirty-five nations on August 1, 1975, in Helsinki, Finland.

8. See the *Journal of the U.S.–U.S.S.R. Trade and Economic Council,* Vol. II, No. 4, 1986, pp. 5–6 for additional commentary on Soviet tourism.

9. For further explanation of the provisions of the National Tourism Policy Act, see "Recent U.S. Tourism Policy Trends," by David L. Edgell, Sr. *International Journal of Tourism Management,* Vol. 3, No. 2, June 1982, pp. 121–23.

10. This section is based on a presentation made by Mindel de la Torre, U.S. Department of Commerce, on May 9, 1989, at the combined seminar of the Tourism Policy Forum (The George Washington University) and the American Bar Association's Subcommittee on Travel and Tourism for the International Service Industries Committee held at the George Washington University. This author also made a presentation on the status of negotiations of the bilateral tourism agreements with Mexico and Venezuela at this seminar. For a summary of the seminar by Milton Zall, see *Tourism Policy Forum Brief,* Vol. 1, No. 3, The George Washington University, Washington, D.C., December 1989.

11. *Journal of Travel Research,* Vol. XXII, No. 3, Winter 1984, pp. 15–16.

12. For a complete discussion of OECD tourism activities on a country-by-country basis, see *Report on Tourism Policy and International Tourism in OECD Member Countries, 1989 Edition,* OECD, Paris, January 1990.

13. "Foreign Policy Implications for Tourism," by David L. Edgell, in *Visions in Leisure and Business,* Vol. 1, Spring 1982, pp. 5–9.

14. An excellent treatment of the details and response to the impact of terrorism on tourism is contained in the article, "International Terrorism: Implications and Challenge for Global Tourism," by Louis J. D'Amore and Teresa E. Anuza, in *Business Quarterly,* Fall 1986. For a clear, concise explanation of the symbiotic relationship between terrorism and tourism, see "Terrorism and Tourism as Logical Companions," by Linda K. Richter and William L. Waugh, Jr., in *Tourism Management,* December 1986.

SUPPLEMENTAL READINGS

Code of Liberalization of Current Invisible Operations. Organization for Economic Cooperation and Development, Paris: December 1976.

Elements of State Policy on Tourism. Salah-Eldin Abdel-Wahab. Italgrafica, Italy, 1974.

The Geography of International Tourism. Ian M. Matley. Washington, D.C.: Association of American Geographers, 1976.

"Goal Programming: Planning Process of Tourism Organization," David L. Edgell, Harvey J. Iglarsh, and Richard L. Seely. *Annals of Tourism Research,* Vol. VII, No. 3, 1980, University of Wisconsin-Stout.

"Inter-American Cooperation in Tourism Training and Research," David L. Edgell. Paper prepared for *The Travel Research Association Conference,* Las Vegas, Nevada, June 7, 1981.

International Business Prospects 1977–1999. Howard F. van Zandt (ed.). Bobbs-Merrill Educational Publisher, Indianapolis, 1978.

Journal of the U.S.–U.S.S.R. Trade and Economic Council, Vol. II, No. 4, 1986, pp. 5–6.

Manila Declaration on World Tourism, World Tourism Conference, Manila, the Philippines, September 27–October 10, 1980.

"New Directions for U.S. National Policy," David L. Edgell and Richard L. Sealy. *International Journal of Tourism Management,* Vol. 1, No. 1, March 1980, pp. 68–69.

The Politics of Tourism in Asia. Linda K. Richter. Honolulu: University of Hawaii Press, 1989.

"Recent U.S. Tourism Policy Trends," David L. Edgell. *International Journal of Tourism Management,* Vol. 3, No. 2, June 1982, pp. 121–123.

Trade Talks: America Better Listen! C. Michael Aho and Jonathan David Aronson. New York: Council on Foreign Relations, 1985.

Visions in Leisure and Business, Vol. 1, Spring 1982, pp. 5–9.

BARRIERS AND OBSTACLES TO INTERNATIONAL TRAVEL

Travel and change of place impart new vigor to the mind.

Lucius Annaeus Seneca, De Tranquillitate Animi, A.D. *60.*

Chapter 1 had a special focus on international tourism within the larger context of worldwide services and showed that services trade was a vibrant array of diverse and fast-growing activities such as tourism. Chapter 2 explained that international tourism was an important and growing commercial and economic activity reaching some 403 million international arrivals and with international tourist receipts of over $208 billion. Chapter 3 implied that the interrelationships of tourism with the world political economy impacted heavily on the growth potential of international tourism.

In this chapter the policy message is that trade in tourism is distorted by a myriad of governmentally imposed quantitative and nonquantitative barriers, which adversely affect the competitive structure of the international travel market and give an unfair advantage to domestic and intraregional travel suppliers.[1] A further observation is that the continued growth of international tourism will depend upon the reduction or elimination of such barriers to international travel worldwide. Such impediments to travel impact on both travelers and travel businesses. While these barriers have been approached separately, both have a major impact on the growth of international tourism and are very often interrelated.[2]

DEFINING BARRIERS TO THE INDIVIDUAL TRAVELER

A number of governmentally imposed impediments to international tourism presently exist. They are numerous and complex and can be looked at in several different ways. They include, for example;

- nontariff barriers: Import-quota-type measures, such as travel allowance restrictions (TARs), which limit the amount of exchange residents of a country may purchase from banks to cover travel expenses incurred abroad; prohibitions on residents' use of credit cards abroad; limitation on duty-free allowances for returning travelers; and advance-import-depositlike measures (i.e., a compulsory deposit a resident of a country must place in escrow, in a non-interest-bearing bank account, for a fixed period of time, before traveling abroad).

- tarifflike measures: Import-duty-type measures, such as an ad valorem tax on foreign exchange purchased to pay for foreign travel or an onerous airport departure or exit tax, that artificially increase the price (to the traveler) of travel services obtained abroad.

- subsidies: Consumer-subsidy-type measures, such as *a.* an official, preferential exchange rate for visiting foreign tourists, which, in effect, enables the visitor to purchase tourism-related services at a lower price than is charged the domestic market and on terms more favorable than those offered in countries whose currencies are on a par with the currency of the subsidizing country; or *b.* price concessions on the cost of admission to tourist attractions, performances, or expositions that are made available by, or at the request of, the national tourist office to visiting foreign tourists, but not to residents.

Travel Allowance Restrictions

Travel allowance restrictions (TARs) limit the value of foreign travel services consumers are able to purchase and wholesalers and retailers are able to sell. Extremely low allowances deter foreign travel altogether.

TARs are probably the most common form of trade barrier confronting the tourism industry internationally and are the most distortive: Once the "allowance" has been spent, foreign suppliers at the destination have no further possibility of selling their services to a traveler, no matter how competitively priced those services may be. In contrast, foreign exchange and exit taxes do not effectively remove foreign competitors from the marketplace; they merely put them at a price disadvantage. Even though they may not be intended to do so, TARs:

- protect domestic tourism industries at the expense of the tourism industries of other countries and

- tend to afford preferential treatment to domestic and intra-regional travel suppliers.

However, they also reduce demand for foreign travel services sold by national airlines and packaged by domestic tour operators and for the counseling and booking services of domestic travel agents who specialize in outbound travel.

More than 100 countries impose TARs. Some prohibit the purchase of exchange for foreign travel altogether. In most instances, however, TARs take the form of a ceiling on the amount of exchange the traveler may purchase from banks and take out of the country to pay for travel services to be procured abroad. In some cases, the ceiling is applied only to exchange for travel to countries outside a given currency area.

Partially as a result of TARs, most international travel today is intraregional. For example, in 1984, the most recent year for which comparative data are available from the World Tourism Organization, intraregional travel accounted for:

- 74 percent of world international tourist arrivals

- 80 percent of international tourist arrivals in Europe

- 69 percent of international tourists arriving in North America

Duty-Free Allowance

Virtually all countries of the world limit the value of items a returning resident or arriving visitor may import free of duty. For example, a U.S. resident who has been out of the country for 48 hours and has not claimed a personal customs exemption within the last 30 days is entitled to a duty-free allowance of $400; an arriving nonresident is entitled to import up to $100 worth of gifts free of duty.

Duty-free allowances are not uniform and vary widely. At least one country has no such allowance and limits the items a returning resident may import free of duty to his baggage and personal effects. Another permits residents to claim the personal customs exemption only once per calendar year. Several countries specify a customs allowance which is below the Customs Cooperation Council Standard ($50).

USTTA's *Inflight Survey* data suggest that low duty-free allowances discourage shopping by tourists and therefore retard the growth of international tourism expenditures. For example, the duty-free allowances for residents of Belgium, Denmark, France, Ireland, Italy, Spain, and the United Kingdom for goods purchased outside the European Community range between $45 and $54. The equivalent allowances for residents of Portugal and Greece are about $25. Survey data show that residents of Europe have the lowest mean expenditure per visitor on gifts and souvenirs of any category of visitor ($224). The allowance for residents of Japan is $1,500, and Japanese have the highest mean expenditure per visitor on gifts and souvenirs of any category of visitor ($576).

Other Restrictions Affecting Travelers

Also relevant to travelers are the restrictions adopted by governments, usually for economic reasons. Limits specified by countries on the amounts that may be spent by travelers in other countries generally are intended to conserve foreign exchange and to defend the country's balance of payments, which is indicative of the economic considerations underlying these limitations. For example, preference sometimes is given to business travelers as opposed to pleasure travelers, thus favoring commerce (regarded as a necessity) over personal consumption (regarded as a luxury).

To illustrate further, sometimes preference is given to tourist expenditures in one currency area over another because of the relative abundance or scarcity of the respective currencies. A dramatic example was that of France in 1983, which adopted temporary restrictions on the number of trips and the amount of money that French citizens could take abroad. Although the restrictions were imposed for balance of payments reasons and were rescinded subsequently, they had a significant effect on tourist earnings of other countries during the crucial summer vacation period that year.

Other restrictions that act as disincentives to travel include, for example, the difficulty of obtaining visa and passport approval, currency restrictions imposed on residents, and travel delays and inconveniences caused by discriminatory treatment of airline ground handling and computer systems. For example, a major restriction on the traveler is the need in some countries to secure a permit called an *exit visa*. In other cases, the government may prohibit purchases of currency for foreign travel—unless the travel is to be to a country, or countries, whose culture, religion, and/or politico economic system is similar to the one of the country of origin.

Taxes on foreign travel sometimes are deliberately designed to discourage outbound travel in favor of domestic travel. This practice is akin to a "buy domestic" policy in merchandise procurement, which generally is regarded as protectionist. In 1982, for example, Indonesia increased its exit tax sixfold for every Indonesian resident traveling abroad. This sharply curtailed the outflow of travelers, particularly the substantial flow of weekend shoppers to Singapore.

Airport/departure taxes and other fees/charges on the traveler cause many visitors to avoid certain destinations or create a negative image that otherwise detracts from a pleasant visit. For example, for many years visitors, airlines, and tourism businesses complained about

Australia's $5 immigration fee and excessive $20 departure tax. A story in the *Sydney Morning Herald,* May 26, 1988 states it this way:

> The Government has caved in to pressure from international airlines and the public and dropped the $5 immigration clearance fee and cut in half the $20 departure tax. . . .
>
> The abolition of the immigration fee was not surprising given the high number of passengers refusing to pay it. . . .
>
> But the reduction of the departure tax to $10 was more surprising and can be seen as a victory for the Minister for Tourism. . . .[3]

This is just one of many such examples, and while there has been no research conducted to measure the results in terms of increased numbers of tourists, Australia has seen recent surges in numbers of visitors.

Other restrictions on travelers may not be monetary, but still may have a major impact on deterring visitors. For example, until recently (1986) the United States had the most restrictive visa system in the world. The U.S. visa requirements had been subject to much criticism from the travel industry. At that time, the United States required that all foreign nationals (with the exception of those from Canada and the Bahamas and United Kingdom nationals resident in Bermuda, the Cayman Islands, and the Turks and Caicos Islands) be in possession of a visa in order to enter the United States as a visitor. This was not a barrier affecting other countries' earnings. On the contrary, it operated as an impediment to U.S. income from foreign visitor expenditures in the United States. Fortunately, in 1986, the Immigration Reform and Control Act was enacted; this Act included a provision to allow a four-year experimental program to waive immigrant visas for up to eight countries. On July 1, 1988, the United Kingdom was chosen as the first experimental country under the law, followed by Japan on December 15, 1988. These two countries were followed by France and Switzerland on July 1, 1989; by the Federal Republic of Germany and by Sweden on July 15, 1989; and by Italy and by the Netherlands on July 29, 1989.

On May 29, 1990, the two responsible Departments for the Visa Waiver Pilot Program, the Departments of State and Justice, sent a report to Congress that:

- evaluates the program;

- finds it highly successful; and

- recommends that it be extended for a further three years and expanded to additional (similar) countries, to be selected by the Attorney General and the Secretary of State.

The program will expire in September 1991 unless Congress approves an extension.

Some Country-Specific Examples

There are so many different kinds of restrictions and barriers to tourism that every country has one or more obstacles or impediments. In an effort to illustrate some of the different kinds of individual country barriers that exist or have existed in the past, a few examples are briefly presented.

- The United States has Customs and Immigration user fees of U.S. $10 (excluding Canada, Mexico, and the Caribbean), which are included in the price of the airline or cruiseline ticket, thus making the international trip more expensive.

- Costa Rica requires nationals and resident foreigners traveling abroad to pay a travel exit tax in Costa Rican *colones* equivalent to about U.S. $10, thus deterring some families from traveling.

- Colombia has a travel allowance restriction for adults of U.S. $180 per day, up to U.S. $3000 per year. A prior deposit of 65 Colombian pesos (25 U.S. cents) per U.S. $1 must be lodged with the Bank of the Republic, refundable within six months upon submission of evidence of amounts actually spent, together with travel documents. This deters and complicates international travel.

- In Korea, until recently, citizens had to be 50 years old or older to obtain a tourist visa, thus restricting younger travelers (unless they were business people) from international travel.

- In Australia, after considerable pressure, the $20 departure tax was reduced to $10, and the $5 immigration fee was finally dropped.

The list of countries and types of restrictions in existence worldwide is so enormous that the real surprise is that international travel is so large; but without such impediments travel would certainly be the largest industry in the world.

OBSTACLES AFFECTING COMPANIES

The prior paragraphs presented a brief description of some of the barriers to individual travelers. In addition, many obstacles affect companies that provide services to facilitate travel. For example, in most countries (the United States is an important exception), travel agents and tour operators are licensed or regulated for the protection of consumers. Licensing practices are designed to promote financial responsibility and to assure that firms deliver the services advertised in a timely manner. When licenses are denied or delayed without good reason, however, the effect is to unfairly limit the competition and to cause disruption in the marketplace. Tour operators, travel agents and others would benefit from the adoption of objective standards based on financial responsibility and past performance, as opposed to rules simply based on nationality.

Government economic policy goals often operate to the disadvantage of foreign-owned travel and tourism businesses. Exchange controls, local equity requirements, labor laws protecting domestic workers, limitations on market access by foreign companies, discriminatory treatment of subsidiaries, inability to utilize computer reservation systems, and restrictions on remittance of earnings tend to discourage the establishment of businesses by foreigners. Investment laws that require minimum ownership by local nationals or place special limitations on foreign investments are intended to promote and protect domestic economic development. Restrictions on the use of foreign-made promotional and advertising materials or taxes on the entry of such information also are intended to stimulate domestic business enterprises. In some countries, tourism promotion offices are established as government monopolies, and private foreign companies are excluded or must enter into an arrangement with a local company, which has full control of the business.

In other countries, "domestic content laws" prevent tourism entities from effectively being able to advertise their tourism products. For example, in Australia, if a tourism commercial contains more than 20 percent foreign material, it must be photographed by Australian film crews. According to the Australian *Financial Review,* September 15, 1989, "This has led to the practice of 'ghost crewing' by Australians, to enable the ad to be shown here."[4]

Tourism involves many different businesses, which are subject to a wide variety of laws and regulations. Many of these regulations are not necessarily designed specifically to afford competitive advantages to the businesses of local nationals, although they may have that effect. The government motivations cited in this section are intended merely to illustrate how international tourist businesses are affected; they do not represent an exhaustive listing of the reasons behind regulations or restrictions.

AIR TRANSPORTATION IMPEDIMENTS

Air transportation policy is a whole separate issue and is not the subject of international tourism policy contained in this book. However, transportation is so integral to the movement of international visitors that certain aspects of air transport policy need to be mentioned at certain junctures in any discussion of tourism policy issues. One such area is the impact of certain problem areas in air transportation that serve to impede traveler or travel-related business.

For example, in the last several years airline passengers have increasingly experienced congestion in air travel. The problem exists from the time the traveler must deal with overcrowding at the airports to flight delays and the concurrent difficulties of security checks, inspection at airports, and general movement of passengers. Other problems inconvenience or hamper travel by air, but the basic point is that innovative solutions must be found if air travel is to increase in the 1990s. With respect to air transportation and problems for travel-related companies, the number-one issue appears to be appropriate interface and access to the various computer reservation systems (CRSs). Computer reservation systems, which began as a simple way to automate the airline ticketing process, have evolved into powerful marketing instruments that have a substantial impact on airline competition and passengers' choice of flights. In the United States, five large CRSs, all owned by major airlines singly or in joint ventures with other carriers, including European airlines, control the market and are regulated by the Department of Transportation. In Europe, two new multi-airline systems, Amadeus and Galileo, have been developed. In Asia and the Pacific, systems called Abacus and Fantasia are the newest CRSs to enter the picture.

CRSs are of increasing potential benefit but they can also be used in such a way as to have a negative impact on the principle of fair competition. There have been many instances where airlines owning CRSs have refused to allow other airlines to participate in their system or have systematically given unfavorable treatment to other airlines when displaying flights or fares. CRSs can also have a negative impact on consumer protection by manipulating information. Carrier participation in CRSs will be a critical issue of the 1990s, but just as important will be the travel agents' relationships with CRSs vendors. The solutions to these problems will have a major impact on international tourism policy.

EXISTING INTERNATIONAL MECHANISMS
FOR REMOVING RESTRICTIONS

As problems arise between countries on matters related to travel and tourism, they are often handled on a bilateral basis (as mentioned in an earlier chapter, the United States, for example, has eight bilateral tourism agreements). However, most of the problems are not limited to a few countries, and thus there is a need for multilateral policy attention at the international level. Several intergovernmental bodies address problems specifically related to tourism and travel, to matters that affect individuals and businesses engaged in tourism, or to activities that have an indirect bearing on tourism.

The work of some organizations relates to travelers and tourist businesses in a broad sense: the OAS, OECD, the WTO, and to a lesser degree, the International Monetary Fund (IMF). Other international organizations, such as the International Civil Aviation Organization (ICAO) and the Customs Cooperation Council (CCC), are more highly specialized in their activities. Problems in international tourism have been addressed in these various forums, mostly in a spirit of cooperation, and in a number of cases, agreements, consensuses, or directions of inquiry have been reached on policy goals and have been adopted in a variety of formal instruments.

Organization for Economic Cooperation and Development (OECD)

The OECD has taken a leadership role in identifying and working toward the reduction of barriers to travel in the twenty-four member countries. In 1979 the OECD Trade Committee initiated an effort to identify and analyze the existing obstacles to trade in services. In view of the major importance of tourism among the principal service industries, it appeared appropriate to the OECD Tourism Committee in 1981 that it should prepare information on tourism services for the Trade Committee. The incentive for such a study was to assemble information that could be utilized by OECD's policymakers on the Committee on Capital Movements and Invisible Transactions (CMIT) for its work on updating and revising the Code of Liberalization of Current Invisible Operations, as well as contributing to the future work of the Tourism Committee itself. Accordingly, the Tourism Committee decided to carry out a survey of obstacles to international tourism and established an Ad Hoc Group to review the material assembled and report such findings to the Tourism Committee. The first report by the Ad Hoc Group was reported to the Tourism Committee in February 1983.[5] At the end of 1983, the Tourism Committee submitted a first comprehensive report to the OECD Council (the policy body of the OECD), "Obstacles to International Tourism in the OECD Area."

A milestone was achieved in efforts to reduce impediments to travel when the OECD Council at its November 1985 meeting approved a new Instrument on International Tourism Policy. The Instrument reaffirmed the importance of tourism to the political, social, and economic well-being of the member countries and agreed to set up formal procedures to identify travel impediments and to take cooperative steps to eliminate them.[6] The special drafting group was chaired by the United States; the overall U.S. particpation in this work was very extensive and was coordinated through the interagency National Tourism Policy Council, chaired by the Secretary of Commerce. U.S. participating agencies in the Council included the Departments of State, Treasury, Transportation, Energy, the Interior, and Labor, the U.S. Trade Representative, the Customs Service, the Immigration and Naturalization Service, Congressional representatives, and other appropriate agencies. Assistance was also provided from such U.S. travel industry groups as the Travel Industry Association of America, the Air Transport Industry Association, the Air Transport Association, the Travel and Tourism Government Affairs Council, and others. Other countries coordinated their efforts in a variety of ways.

The OECD tourism instrument recommended minimum amounts for the import and export of national currency, for travel allowances, and for duty-free allowances for returning residents and for nonresidents, as well as recommendations concerning travel documents and other formalities, striving towards facilitation of tourism. A recent OECD survey, for example, found that the most numerous highly rated concerns among the countries responding were those impediments related to market access and the right of establishment. This reflects the importance of reaching customers in the country of residence in order to attract tourist and travel business. Without a local branch or subsidiary, travel agents, tour operators, airlines, and other tourist companies are unable to market their services adequately, thus placing them at a competitive disadvantage.

Through its Tourism Committee and various other committees, including those that administer codes on capital movements and invisible operations, the OECD is playing a constructive role in addressing the impediments to international trade in tourism. The Tourism Committee recently (1988) completed an extensive review of obstacles to all aspects of tourism in member countries. The committee may possibly seek to expand the work to examine obstacles in nonmember countries as well. Actions to seek removal or reduction of obstacles in nonmember countries would improve the total world travel market. New instruments and more aggressive enforcement of current provisions are needed. At some point, to achieve global effectiveness, the OECD's work would have to be referred to other international bodies. Because the OECD generally focuses on broader economic issues, the value of this exercise within the organization will need to be recognized and given high priority.

World Tourism Organization (WTO)

The World Tourism Organization has a Facilitation Committee whose aims are to propose measures to simplify entry and exit formalities, report on existing governmental requirements or practices that may impede the development of international travel, and develop a set of standards and recommended practices for a draft convention to be presented to member states for adoption. The WTO has developed a set of standards and recommended practices on passports and visas, is working on a model convention on passports and visas, and is studying exchange control practices.

In addition, the WTO annually issues the publication *Travel Abroad—Frontier Formalities*. This publication contains information on current rules and practices—in the areas of passports and visas, customs formalities and facilities, health regulations, currency formalities and facilities, and temporary importation of vehicles— applicable to nonimmigrant travelers crossing the frontiers of some 170 countries and territories. Recently (with the 1988 edition), this publication added some general AIDS information for travelers. This one-page section strongly suggests that "concerns about AIDS should not prevent travel to any part of the world." In addition, every two years the WTO issues a "Biennial Report Concerning the Situation of Facilitation in the World," which reports on police formalities applicable to travelers, customs allowances, health formalities, currency allowances, passport and visa regulations, and international agreements on the security and legal protection of travelers.

WTO has the broadest scope of any international organization dealing with travel and tourism issues. The organization's main work emphasis has been on the promotion and facilitation of tourism and the dissemination of information and statistics. The WTO also sponsors special workshops and conferences on a wide variety of tourism subjects, from a Workshop on Environmental Aspects of Tourism to others dealing with special topics, as for example the International Conference on Statistics scheduled for 1991. In 1986, it addressed impediments in the business environment that hamper the development of tourism-related firms in foreign countries and thereby limit travel and the sale of the tourist product internationally. To follow through on this initiative, the WTO established a Facilitation Committee.

International Monetary Fund (IMF)

The IMF, located in Washington D.C., provides loans to member countries and exercises surveillance over exchange rate policies and the international monetary system. The organization publishes an important *Annual Report on Exchange Controls and Exchange*

Restrictions. The report has various sections that provide a detailed description of the exchange and trade system of individual member countries, many of which explain restrictive systems that impact on international travel. Some of the issues dealt with are described in the next paragraph.

Currency exchange and controls imposed by governments can constitute significant obstacles to tourism-related businesses. Restrictions or limits on the remittance of profits and transfer of funds serve to impede the establishment of foreign-owned tourism businesses in various countries. Delays in currency conversion, particularly for credit card companies and others engaged in providing financial services for travelers, act as impediments to commerce and tourism. Airlines, for example, have sometimes had large sums tied up in soft-currency countries.[7]

The IMF influences exchange controls and financial policy on a global basis. In annual consultations with member countries, the IMF, as appropriate, pressures countries to liberalize their exchange restrictions commensurate with improvements in economic conditions.

International Civil Aviation Organization (ICAO)

The International Civil Aviation Organization (Montreal), consisting of about 150 member countries, addresses a wide variety of air transport issues, promulgating international standards and recommended practices regulating air navigation. The bulk of the recommended practices deal with the safety, regulation, and efficiency of air navigation, as well as customs and immigration procedures. The organization also reviews restrictive standards that discriminate against nonnational tour businesses and against nonnational airlines in establishing ground handling facilities and computerized reservation systems.

Facilitation of international tourism is so important for the ICAO members that at the September 1988 ICAO Conference on Facilitation some important recommendations were made.

- Improvement of access to airports for elderly and disabled passengers

- Harmonization of security and facilitation objectives

- Development of machine-readable passports and visas

- The use of dual-channel systems to expedite baggage clearance

Other issues that impact on the flow of passengers through air transport systems were dealt with as well.

Customs Cooperation Council (CCC)

The Customs Cooperation Council, in Brussels, composed of more than ninety countries, reviews issues relating to customs procedures, classification and valuation of goods, and harmonization and simplification of customs practices. It seeks to attain the highest degree of harmony and uniformity in national customs systems.

The International Convention on the Simplification and Harmonisation of Customs Procedures, approved in Kyoto by the CCC in 1973, contains an annex on customs facilities applicable to travelers. By May 1986, seven countries—Algeria, Finland, Israel, Kenya, Rwanda, Switzerland, and the United States—had accepted the annex with certain reservations and/or exceptions.

While the CCC activities are more narrowly defined, facilitation of customs procedures and standardized customs approaches in expediting passenger travel is important to the growth of tourism.

HOW EFFECTIVE ARE THE EXISTING MECHANISMS?

Worldwide tourism has managed to grow despite the numerous and various impediments to travelers and travel businesses. Continued growth is projected, but few studies have projected the higher level of international travel that could be attained in the absence of restrictive practices. Some increases, of course, could only be achieved on a limited bilateral level, and there are obvious limits to growth imposed by the limited purchasing power in some countries. Moreover, there is no assurance that new barriers will not be erected in individual countries in the future. The potential for government-imposed restrictions increases as economic conditions worsen and competition for tourism sharpens.

On the other hand, recent improvements in the world economy have set the stage for realization of the mass-market potential of tourism. The vast majority of the world's people have not traveled beyond the borders of their homeland or neighboring countries. Reduction or removal of barriers would help to stimulate the development of tourism and would make it easier to market and promote to this segment of the world's population.

Nearly all the problems discussed above have been addressed by governments in some way, whether unilaterally, bilaterally, or multilaterally. However, the fact that many problems remain is an indication that further work is necessary. Moreover, the relatively large number of international organizations with jurisdiction over limited aspects of tourism would seem to indicate that what is lacking is an overall international plan with clear objectives and widespread general support by governments.

The work of the IMF is heavily concentrated on exchange rate and financial stability; facilitation of trade and tourism are of only secondary interest. The OECD and the WTO currently devote more attention to the broad range of impediments to travelers and travel businesses. However, the OECD is limited by its relatively small number of member countries, and the WTO is not equipped with staff and legal means to implement and enforce country compliance with adopted standards. In short, there is no single organization that can be looked to for resolution of these problems in the nineties, with possibly one exception.

General Agreement on Tariffs and Trade (GATT)

Given the number of existing international organizations with overlapping jurisdiction over various aspects of tourism, it is natural to ask why yet another organization, the GATT, should be enlisted to deal with the same types of problems.

The GATT covers the world's major industrialized and developing countries. Although many trade problems remain and much work is needed to strengthen GATT rules and operations, the organization has a good track record in reducing tariff barriers on merchandise trade over the last four decades. GATT's work on nontariff barriers has only begun in recent years, and this is an area that needs special attention. The impediments to tourism and other services correspond in many ways to the nontariff barriers on merchandise trade.

The organization has developed an internationally recognized set of rules and procedures for consultations and dispute settlements and has a highly professional staff. Perhaps no other international body has more experience in dealing with technical issues and practical situations that hamper international commerce.

Presently, a potential window of opportunity for multilateral discussions on barriers to trade in tourism exists. In early September 1986, at the ocean resort town of Punta del Este, Uruguay, ninety-two member ministers of trade of the GATT met and concluded the *Ministerial Declaration on the Uruguay Round*. This agreement provides, for the first time ever, a section on "Negotiations on Trade in Services." Over the years (since its establishment in 1948), the GATT has managed to reduce many barriers to trade in goods. If, under the auspices of the new Uruguay Round of talks, tourism, as part of services, were included in the current GATT talks in Geneva, there might be a better opportunity than currently exists for reducing barriers to international tourism.[8]

Using GATT as the mechanism for dealing with trade-in-tourism barriers has been gaining some support. The WTO Commission for Europe Special Committee on Tourism and the GATT has prepared a study concerning the inclusion of tourism and tourist services in the GATT negotiations.[9] One of the agreements to support the concept of GATT negotiations on the liberalization of services is that trade in services in general, and tourism in particular, could be expanded if the economic, legal, and nontariff restrictions did not exist. Generally, the WTO has been encouraging and working with GATT to include tourism in the current GATT negotiations. Similarly, the OAS at its Inter-American Travel Congress meeting in 1988 passed a resolution supporting the inclusion of tourism barriers in the GATT talks. The article "Trade Group Discussions: Tourism and Travel" in *The New York Times,* July 24, 1989, states that "International talks intended to reduce protectionism in tourism and transportation began last week, with much enthusiasm for change but a widespread reluctance to dismantle barriers."[10]

Whether the GATT decides to take up barriers to tourism in its negotiation process is still unknown. But certainly the GATT offers the greatest potential opportunity for reducing travel barriers that currently exist, and only time will tell whether this organization or some other body will make progress on this important policy issue.

Coordination of International Organizations

Considering the multiplicity of international organizations dealing with the various aspects of tourism and travel, attempts to achieve liberalization or to develop codes of conduct will require interaction of organizations. If tourism is to be treated as an integral unit, these international organizations will have to work together more closely, relying on the expertise of specialized agencies and, as necessary, referring issues or recommendations to other bodies. Without an overall organized approach to tourism, matters will continue to be handled on a fragmented basis, and some of the impetus for accelerated liberalization will be lost.

The effect of multilateral trade negotiations on travel and tourism businesses will depend upon the scope of the negotiations: whether tourism is treated as an individual sector, how tourism will be defined, and what element of tourism will be included. The outcome also will be determined by many other factors: the interrelation with negotiations on other service sectors, how countries perceive their own interests being served, finding mutuality of interests, and the views expressed by businesses in the various countries.

As with all trade negotiations, the parties will need to do a great deal of soul-searching, carefully weighing the estimated benefits and costs, including the degree of discomfort that results when governments limit their freedom of action (such as balance-of-payments actions) by tying themselves to legally binding international rules. There must be some willingness to accept obligations in order to gain reciprocal benefits from other countries. It is equally important that business groups, interested in maximum flows of, and purchases by, travelers and tourists, should express their views and encourage their governments to find ways of removing or progressively reducing barriers to international tourism.

NOTES

1. A comprehensive discussion of impediments to trade in tourism was dealt with in the article, "Barriers to International Travel," by Bernard Ascher and David L. Edgell, in *Travel and Tourism Analyst,* October 1986. Also see "Obstacles to International Travel and Tourism," by Bernard Ascher, in *Journal of Travel Research,* Vol. XXII, No. 3, Winter 1984.

2. This section relies heavily on the article referred to in Note 1 and on a discussion of "Barriers to International Travel in the Americas," by David L. Edgell, *Tourism Management,* March 1988, pp. 63–66. See also the *U.S. National Study on Trade in Services,* U.S. Government Printing Office, Washington, D. C., 1984; *Travel Information Manual,* IATA member airlines, August 1989; and *Exchange Arrangement and Exchange Restrictions Annual Report 1989*; International Monetary Fund, Washington, D.C., 1989.

3. For a more complete explanation of Australia's action in reducing the departure tax, see "Departure Tax Halved, Fee Dropped," by Ross Dunn, in *The Sydney Morning Herald,* May 26, 1988.

4. An interesting exposé on this issue is in "Hollywood Attacks Australian Content TV Rule," by Anne Davies, in the Australian *Financial Review,* September 15, 1989.

5. The full report of the OECD Tourism Committee's Ad Hoc Group studying tourism barriers is included as Chapter V, "Obstacle to International Tourism in the OECD Area," in *Tourism Policy and International Tourism,* OECD, Paris, 1984, pp. 68–79.

6. Additional information about other aspects of OECD's work on tourism impediments can be found in the article, "Travel and Tourism: OECD Countries Move to Eliminate Travel Obstacles," by Albert N. Alexander, in *Business America,* U.S. Department of Commerce, February 17, 1986, p. 19.

7. For a full account of some of the country-by-country restrictions impacting on international travel, see the *Exchange Arrangements and Exchange Restrictions Annual Report 1989,* International Monetary Fund, July 1989.

8. For an explanation of some of the reasons why GATT appears as the logical choice for resolving barriers issues in the Americas, see "Barriers to International Travel in the Americas," by David L. Edgell, in *Tourism Management,* March 1988, pp. 63–66.

9. See "WTO Commission for Europe Special Committee on Tourism and the GATT" report in an *Information Document* by WTO, Madrid, September 1988.

10. This interesting article discusses the fact that tourism is a very major industry and the GATT is reviewing the facts for inclusion of tourism.

SUPPLEMENTAL READINGS

"Barriers to International Travel." Bernard Ascher and David L. Edgell. *Travel and Tourism Analyst (The Economic Publications),* London, October 1986, pp. 3–13

"Barriers to International Travel in the Americas." David L. Edgell. *Tourism Management,* March 1988.

Exchange Arrangements and Exchange Restrictions Annual Report 1989. International Monetary Fund, Washington, D.C., 1989.

"Obstacles to International Tourism in the OECD Area." *Tourism Policy and International Tourism,* Organization for Economic Cooperation and Development, Paris, 1984, pp. 68–79.

"Obstacles to International Travel and Tourism." Bernard Ascher. *Journal of Travel Research,* Vol. XXII, No. 3, Winter 1984.

"Travel and Tourism: OECD Countries Move to Eliminate Travel Obstacles." Albert N. Alexander. *Business America,* Washington, D.C. February 17, 1986, p. 19.

The Travel Industry (2nd ed.). Chuck Y. Gee, James C. Makens, and Dexter J. L. Choy. New York: Van Nostrand Reinhold, 1989, pp. 84–94.

Travel Information Manual. A Joint Publication of Fourteen International Air Transport Association member airlines, printed in the Netherlands, Van Boekhoven-Bosch, B. V., Utrecht, August 1989.

U.S. National Study on Trade in Services. U.S. Government Printing Office, Washington, D.C. 1984.

World Tourism Organization Commission for Europe Special Committee on Tourism and the GATT, Madrid, Spain, September 1988.

5

SOCIOCULTURAL AND ENVIRONMENTAL ASPECTS OF INTERNATIONAL TOURISM

A guest never forgets the host who had treated him kindly.

Homer, The Odyssey, 9th century B.C.

One of the most important motivations for travel is interest in the culture of other people in other countries. Sociocultural and environmental aspects of international tourism relate to the way people learn about each other's way of life, thoughts, and interactions with the environment. When a visitor has a positive cultural experience in a pleasant environment he won't forget "the host who had treated him kindly."

There are representative expressions of people and places that provide powerful attractions for travel. People are interested in languages, expressions, cultures, and environments that are different from their own. Culture may include art, music, painting, sculpture, and architecture as well as special events, celebrations, and festivals. Or the cultural attraction may be food, drink, entertainment, or some other special form of hospitality. The environment might be built with significant cultural, historical, or hospitality orientation, or it might be a natural landscape, a pleasant seashore, a magnificent mountain, or lovely forest—or it simply might be the social interactions of human beings. The concern here is to recognize that such experiences may be positive, or in some circumstances negative, and to recognize the need for policy guidance to ensure that the future growth of tourism will allow for a balanced tourism experience.

The current rapid growth and development of tourism puts a special pressure on sociocultural and environmental planning. All too frequently there are complaints that tourism generates pollution, crowding, crime, prostitution, and the corruption of the language, culture, and customs of some local populations. This chapter will explore some of the negative and positive aspects of sociocultural and environmental issues in tourism.

SOCIOCULTURAL PROBLEMS

It is clear that tourism has, in a short time-frame, led to a closer association and mingling of people of different races, creeds, religions, and cultures. However, there is a growing concern that mass international tourism may have a detrimental impact on local cultures and customs or that a local area will distort its local festivals and ceremonies to stage spectacles for the benefit of international visitors. Thus, to some people tourism leads to the disappearance of traditional human environments, replaces them with towers of artificial concrete, ideas, ethics, and morals, and in effect threatens the whole fabric of tradition and nature.[1] In addition, there is concern that as such distortions arise, the host and guest become a part of separate worlds, leading to even greater prejudices and misunderstandings. For example, in the book *The Golden Hordes,* Turner and Ash contend that modern tourism is a form of cultural imperialism, an unending pursuit of fun, sun, and sex by the golden hordes of pleasure seekers who are damaging local cultures and polluting the world in their quest. In brief, the authors feel that a lot of "tourism" damages the local culture of the host country, perverts the traditional social values, encourages prostitution and hustling among "the natives," and usually results in a proliferation of fabricated tourist-oriented cultural performances and the sale of cheap souvenirs masquerading as local arts and crafts.[2]

In other articles it is frequently mentioned that the attitude of the local population toward tourists is sometimes hostile, due to the tourists' outlandish requirements for accommodations and services or due to the unreasonable wants and demands of a limited number of rude and arrogant visitors. Other problems cited include the fact that in many of the developing countries there is foreign ownership and management of tourist facilities, which may create the feeling that indigenous people perform only menial tasks. Tourism may be regarded as a threat to the indigenous culture and mores. There is often a perception that tourists are mainly responsible for the deterioration in standards of local arts and crafts as efforts are made to expand output to meet tourists' demands. And, not infrequently, resort development has resulted in local people being denied access to their own beaches. All these factors can give rise to serious problems in the perception of tourists and sometimes to demands for limitations on the flow of visitors.

AVOIDING SOCIOCULTURAL PROBLEMS

While certainly there are numerous incidents where tourism does impact negatively on an area, this does not have to happen. A carefully planned, well-organized tourist destination can benefit the residents through exposure to a variety of ideas, people, languages, and other cultural traits in addition to economic benefits. It can add to the richness of a resident's experience by stimulating an interest in the area's history through restoration and preservation of historical sites.

For example, some of the cultural richness in the U.S. black communities is being revived as potential for tourism development.[3] In New York, the revitalization of Harlem has made that community a well-known tourist destination abroad. The myths, realities, folklore, and legacies of Harlem are now known around the world. It is increasingly being recognized both domestically and internationally for its rich cultural heritage, landmarks, museums, churches, parks, architectural structures, and varied nightlife.[4]

Organized cultural tourism development can provide opportunities for local people to learn more about themselves, thus increasing feelings of pride in their heritage and a heightened perception of their own worth. For example, residents of Mexico City speak with great pride about their Ballet Folklorico, their National Museum of Anthropology, and their Palace of Fine Arts. The Venezuelans speak lovingly and affectionately about "La Feria de San Sebastian," a great festive event with cultural and other exciting celebrations that not only results in Venezuelan participation but includes foreign interest and visitation as well.[5]

Even a highly localized heritage event such as "Buffalo Bill Cody Days," a festive occasion wherein the residents of Leavenworth, Kansas, celebrate their historical link to William F. (Buffalo Bill) Cody (1846–1917), can be a positive cultural experience for nonresidents as well.[6] The local celebration of "Potomac Days Parade" in Potomac, Maryland, is an event that has grown into an international festival where people of many different heritages ranging from Korea to Lithuania show off traditional clothes, food, and arts and crafts.[7] These local celebrations started gradually but have grown into regular yearly celebrations that both residents and visitors look forward to.

Tourism can also contribute to cultural revival. Often, the demand by tourists for local arts and crafts has heightened the interest and maintained the skills of local artisans and craftsmen by providing an audience and market for their art. In the United States, a number of Indian ceremonies and dances owe much of their continued existence to the fact that tourists were interested in them. This stimulated many local Indians to revive and teach to the new generations the meaning of such traditions. This preservation of cultural heritage, whether it be in local artifacts, historic sites, or religious rites, forms the heritage of an area or country. Often, this very uniqueness is the primary tourism attraction. It is a contribution to the quality of life of both the residents and tourists. But it is often the tourists who provide the interest and economic means to preserve and maintain this cultural heritage.

The Manila Declaration (from the World Tourism Conference held in Manila in 1980) summarizes tourism's contribution to sociocultural and environmental benefits as follows:

> The protection, enhancement and improvement of various components of man's environment are among the fundamental conditions for the harmonious development of tourism. Similarly, rational management of tourism may contribute to a large extent to protecting and developing the physical environment and the cultural heritage as well as improving the quality of life . . . tourism brings people closer together and creates an awareness of the diversity of ways of life, traditions and aspirations. . . .[8]

In other words, the sociocultural and environmental aspects of an area can enrich tourism in general and provide different and unique opportunities for tourists to experience arts, music, dance, food, literature, language, religion, and history different from their own. At the same time, tourists bring to the local area sociocultural traits from their homeland. This cross-cultural manifestation can have positive or negative results, depending on the way tourism is planned and handled in the receiving country.

For many years, the OAS has been concerned with the need to enhance the positive aspects of the sociocultural and environmental impacts of tourism (particularly in the Caribbean). The numerous studies and reports by the OAS outline potential approaches for a better understanding of the issues involved. In addition, the WTO has taken a strong interest in sociocultural and environmental concerns for tourism. The WTO General Assembly, which met in Sofia, Bulgaria (September 1985), adopted a *Tourism Bill of Rights and Tourist Code,* which contains several articles outlining sociocultural concerns in tourism. Two brief excerpts suffice to illustrate the importance of this issue:

> [Article VI] "They (host communities) are also entitled to expect from tourists understanding and respect for their customs, religions and other elements of their cultures which are part of the human heritage. . . .
>
> [Article VII] "The population constituting the host communities in place of transit and sojourn are invited to receive tourists with the greatest possible hospitality, courtesy and respect necessary for the development of harmonious human and social relations. . . ."[9]

Another Code dealing with cultural aspects of tourism was developed in 1975 by the Christian Conference of Asia. A report to this Conference on "Tourism, the Asian Dilemma," as edited by Ron O'Grady, reads as follows:

A Code of Ethics for Tourists

- Travel in a spirit of humility and with a genuine desire to learn more about the people of your host country.

- Be aware of the feelings of other people, thus preventing what might be offensive behavior on your part. This caution applies very much to photography.

- Cultivate the habit of listening and observing rather than merely hearing and seeing.

- Realize that often the people in the country you visit have time concepts and thought patterns different from your own; these differences do not make them inferior, only different.

- Instead of looking for the "beach paradise," discover the enrichment of seeing a different way of life through other eyes.

- Acquaint yourself with local customs; people will be happy to help you.

- Instead of adhering to the Western practice of "knowing all the answers," cultivate the habit of asking questions.

- Remember that you are only one of the thousands of tourists visiting this country; do not expect special privileges.

- If you really want your experience to be "a home away from home," it is foolish to waste money on traveling.

- When you are shopping, remember that the "bargain" you obtained was possible only because of the low wages paid to the maker.

- Do not make promises to people in your host country unless you are certain you can carry them through.

- Spend time reflecting on your daily experiences in an attempt to deepen your understanding. It has been said that "what enriches you may rob and violate others."[10]

This code and related concerns by certain church groups seek to support greater authenticity in cultural tourism. There are some advocates for greater involvement by churches in local community planning in order to sensitize tourists to a greater understanding of local cultures.

In planning for international visitors, the host country must understand the great sociocultural variety in the backgrounds of the visitors as well as their reasons for the visit. Many people want the excitement of visiting new and different areas of the world, but at the same time they may be apprehensive about strange languages, customs, and social structures. Salah Wahab in his book, *Tourism Management*, has one prescription for this paradox. He states: "The tourist country should be sufficiently different to be exciting and diversified, offering the tourist the novelty and escape he seeks, but sufficiently similar in comfort and security conditions to the tourist's own country to make him feel relaxed and at ease."[11] Certainly one of the challenges for planning a balanced tourism product is being able to take into account the sociocultural wants and needs of the visitor, balanced with positive attributes for the host.

SOME SPECIAL CASES OF HERITAGE TOURISM

Some communities seek to restore old buildings and similar edifices in an effort to maintain the historic preservation of the area and to draw visitors to participate in the local cultural heritage. In addition, there are examples, like Williamsburg, Virginia, where the complete community is a replica of its history and culture. Still others, like the Polynesian Culture Center in Hawaii, seek to create visitor interest through the performance of dances and rituals of several different cultures in one place. While these efforts are often applauded, there are also many detractors who are critical and suggest that such portrayals are artificial substitutes and often demean the society and culture on display.

An excellent example of a monumental effort to preserve a cultural, historical, and environmental heritage through tourism is the five-nation regional project referred to as *La Ruta Maya*—the Maya Route. In an eighty-one-page article in the October 1989 issue of *National Geographic,* author and editor Wilbur E. Garrett explains in great detail the opportunity that La Ruta Maya offers to "increase environmentally oriented tourism and sustainable, nondestructive development to provide jobs and money to help pay for preservation." To get five countries—Mexico, Belize, Guatemala, Honduras, and El Salvador—all to agree to cooperate in this ambitious regional project provides a model for other parts of the world.[12]

Heritage tourism appears to be gaining widespread acceptance both as a part of the overall tourism effort and separately as a special attraction. Like other aspects of sociocultural tourism, heritage tourism often creates a source of community pride that helps to ease resentment toward visitors and to prevent displacement of residents' businesses, particularly in downtown areas, which often need economic revitalization and often present an opportunity for cultural enrichment. The key is to balance the complaints of local residents about such problems as traffic congestion and lack of parking brought on by visitors with the economic benefits and the potential for community pride in culture. It takes strong leadership and community support to overcome the obstacles and to explain the benefits that tourism can bestow on a local area. In summary, a well-planned effort can reap the economic benefits, preserve buildings of historic significance, and create community pride in what the community offers to locals and outsiders alike.

There is no question that cultural tourism is an integral part of international tourism and is growing as global tourism expands. Estimates are that between 20 and 25 percent of international visitors are interested in a cultural experience while traveling internationally.[13] Part and parcel of the cultural experience in tourism is its relationship to the local environment. Cultural tourism relates both directly and indirectly to environmental concerns. There are other questions with respect to tourism and the environment that have very little bearing on cultural tourism. The next section will look at tourism and the environment from a broad perspective that may or may not relate to cultural interrelationships.

THE ENVIRONMENT

Pleasant climates, scenic wonders, beautiful coastlines and beaches, majestic mountains and valleys, rugged woods interspersed with rolling plains, magnificent skylines, and rhythmic sounds of the sea are all part of the natural environmental attractions that cause large movements of people worldwide. In addition, the human environment, which includes lodging, transportation, attractions, museums, art galleries, and many more, is a major part of the international tourism scene. The key is to balance the numbers of visitors with capacities of the given environments in a way which allows for the greatest interaction with the least destruction. There are many differences of opinion on how this can best be accomplished.

Concerns for the Environment

Numerous recent happenings suggest that tourists and the environment are not very compatible. Some tourists want souvenirs such as special corals, exotic rocks, or lots of seashells. Others trample irreplaceable tundra or otherwise alter natural flora and fauna. Some people may want to chip off a piece of the Colosseum, walk off with native artifacts, or otherwise desecrate important objects of historical and artistic importance.

The environment in which tourism interacts is broad in scope, including not only land, air, water, flora, and fauna but also the human environment. The physical environment is just one facet of the surroundings with which the tourist comes in contact. As mentioned earlier, the tourist also must relate to sociocultural differences as well. In brief, the environment in its broad definition is what attracts the tourist in the first place. It may be the ecosystem, the wildlife, the rich archeological discoveries, the climate, or the culture that the tourist may have read about, seen on the movie or television screen, or been told about by a friend. The important note is that whatever the environment, it must be protected as an inheritance for future generations of visitors.

Recent commentaries paint a bleak picture for tourism's interaction with the environment. In an article titled, "Will There Be Any Nice Places Left?" a number of negative aspects of worldwide tourism are presented.[14] Polluted beaches, urban blight, eroded landscapes, and sprawling slumlike developments are mentioned as frequent sights in tourism areas. Many tourism developments are demeaning to local residents, overcrowded, noisy, conducive to traffic congestion, architecturally tasteless, and an overload on the infrastructure. Much of this kind of development in the past has been due to laissez-faire tourism policies and a lack of national, regional, or local planning.

In recent years, interest in the impact of tourism on the environment has been increasing. The discussion has dwelt more on environmental degradation caused by tourism than on positive aspects of tourism. The report of the 1973 European Travel Commission Conference on Tourism and Conservation stated rather forcefully both the positive and negative factors in the interdependent relationship between tourism and the environment:

> First, . . . environment is the indispensable basis, the major attraction for tourism. Without an attractive environment there would be no tourism. . . .
> Second, . . . the interests of tourism demand the protection of the scenic and historic heritage. The offer in the travel brochure must be genuine. . . .
> In some countries, tourism . . . is seen by those concerned to protect the environment as their powerful ally. The desire to gain national income from tourism can impel governments to protect monuments or natural areas they might otherwise have neglected. . . .
> Third, tourism can directly assist active conservation . . . can prompt men

to contribute towards. . . . conservation . . . of [famous places such as] Florence and . . . Venice. The entry fees of tourists help to maintain historic structures and parks. . . . Tourist activity may provide new uses for old buildings. . . .

And yet, despite these positive links, many conservationists feel that tourism can present a major threat to the environment . . . that countless hotels, roads and other facilities provided for the tourists ruin the beauties of the seacoast, disturb the peace of the country, and rob the mountains of their serene grandeur . . . streets [are] choked with tourist traffic, and . . . squares and marketplaces turned into parks for visitors.[15]

For Europe, the relationship between tourism and the environment seemed to grow steadily worse throughout the 1970s. In an article from *The Washington Post,* August 3, 1985, "Tourism Found Mixed Blessing by World Group," many of the negative features of tourism and the environment were highlighted based on an OECD survey. The article made the point that Europe had not been forceful in maintaining a balance between tourism and the environment.[16]

A further example of environmental-tourism issues already being faced in Europe is the congestion problem in Venice. In "Venice Overwhelmed by Holiday Weekend Visitors; City May Restrict Entry," in *Tour and Travel News,* May 11, 1987, it is pointed out that Venice is so "overwhelmed" by tourists that on May 2, 1989, the bridge connecting Venice to the mainland was closed. The pedestrian traffic became so burdensome that the police were compelled to ask tourists to show proof of hotel reservations before they could enter.[17] Another example is cited in the article, "Apocalypse in the Alps," in *Time* magazine, September 3, 1984. This article points out the congestion problems in Alpine ski areas during the ski season.[18] The overload on the natural and built environments in some areas of the Alps is already beyond capacity. It has only been recently that substantive solutions to such problems have come to the fore.

And you do not have to go to Europe to find conflicts of tourism and the environment. Closer to home, in the Galapagos Islands (Ecuador), there are problems with overvisitation. "Tourism, Immigration Put Strain on Galapagos," in *The Washington Post,* March 19, 1987, explains problems that arise with too many people living and visiting in a fragile environment.[19] Further problems exist in Puerto Rico with respect to polluted beaches. "Dirty Beaches Remain Problem for the Tourism Industry," in *Caribbean Business,* November 12, 1989, explains some of the debris left behind by residents and tourists and its negative impact on the beaches.[20] A similar situation exists in many beach areas on the mainland U.S. from New Jersey to Texas to California. "Our Befouled Beaches," in *Newsweek,* July 27, 1987, tells the awful story of polluted beaches in these states.[21]

Some Positive Movement

More recently, people have become increasingly concerned about all aspects of pollution—whether it be industrial, noise, people, visual, or tourism development. Even though most of the evidence suggests that the development of tourism infrastructure and facilities has generally caused less physical environmental damage than have timber and mineral extractions or industrial plants, there is concern for tourism development impacts on the environment in some areas. This concern has given rise to developmental constraints in an attempt to preserve the ecosystem and improve the quality of the environment. This recognition and protection has important benefits for the long-run health of the tourism industry. Without the protection of the scenic splendor that is often the very attraction to the tourist, the quality of tourism will deteriorate.

Current efforts in the United States range from small individual projects through efforts of local conservation-oriented groups to broad national policies. A clear explanation of the latter was contained in "Visitor Limits Planned in Some National Parks," in *The Washington Post* (June 8, 1985), which discusses new rules by the National Park Service to preserve natural resources. The article points out that in 1960 there were 26.6 million visits to the national parks. By 1983, this had increased to 63.8 million visits. In response to the potential "long-range environmental damage from intense human use . . . the National Park Service . . . will shut the gates of some major parks during busy vacation periods to restrict access and reduce human impact on the parks' original inhabitants."[22]

The Challenge

The preceding paragraphs demonstrate that the sociocultural and environmental impacts of tourism need not be negative. To the contrary, we can argue that there is a very natural interdependence between tourism and the culture and environment of a country. This concept was most eloquently addressed in a speech by the President of India, Giani Zail Singh, before the General Assembly of the World Tourism Organization in New Delhi on October 3, 1983. He said:

> Tourism can become a vehicle for the realization of man's highest aspirations in the quest for knowledge, education, understanding, acceptance and affirmation of the originality of cultures, and respect for the moral heritage of different peoples. I feel that it is these spiritual values of tourism that are significant. . . . Tourism has also made it possible for nations to develop strategies for the conservation of natural and cultural heritage of mankind. Planning for economic growth and development must go hand in hand with

the protection of environment, enhancement of cultural life, and maintenance of rich traditions which contribute so greatly to the quality of life and character of a nation. The rapid and sometimes alarming deterioration of the environment due to pollution which is entirely man-made must be a matter for concern to all of us, who hold in trust on behalf of our peoples, the distinctive heritage of our respective countries. . . .[23]

To obtain this aspect of an improved "quality of life" is a challenge for tourism, particularly in the next ten years. It will not "just happen." It will have to become an integral part of the policy and planning process for tourism development.

For example, if properly organized, tourism can provide an incentive for the protection of national parks, the restoration of historical monuments, and the preservation of cultural events. In many places in the world, the expenditures made by tourists are the economic means to protect the environment. For example, in a story in *U.S. News and World Report,* May 4, 1987, Bruce Wilson from the Center for Conservation Biology at Stanford University said: "What has saved gorillas and cheetahs in Africa is the prospect of $500 million a year from safari-bound tourists."[24]

MEETING THE CHALLENGE

The 1960s were a basis for the concerns about the environment that are now the foundation for much of the policy formulation with respect to current tourism development. For example, the United Nations Conference on the Human Environment held in Stockholm, Sweden, in 1972 summed up some of the issues of the 1960s and emphasized the need to identify and combat environmental problems in the early stages of tourism planning and development.[25] By 1980 considerable discussion had been generated about tourism and the environment. This concern was summed up in the Manila Declaration on World Tourism as follows:

Tourism resources available in the various countries consist at the same time of space, facilities and values. These are resources whose use cannot be left uncontrolled without running the risk of their deterioration, or even their destruction. The satisfaction of tourism requirements must not be prejudicial to the social and economic interests of the population in tourist areas, to the environment, or above all, to natural resources, which are the fundamental attraction of tourism, and historical and cultural sites. All tourism resources are part of the heritage of mankind. National communities and the entire international community must take the necessary steps to ensure their preservation.[26]

This Declaration was further reinforced when on July 1, 1982, the World Tourism Organization and the United Nations Environment Programs signed a joint agreement affirming that:

> The protection, enhancement and improvement of the various components of man's environment are among the fundamental conditions for the harmonious development of tourism. Similarly, national management of tourism may contribute to a large extent to protecting and developing the physical environment and the cultural heritage, as well as to improving the quality of man's life. . . . [Nations should seek] to promote, establish and implement a strategy and a program of concerted actions designed to ensure balance between the development of holiday and travel activities, which should be considered irreversible, and the protection of the environment, whose components constitute the common heritage of mankind.[27]

In addition to these multinational declarations on tourism and the environment, there are numerous examples of positive approaches taken by individual countries. Probably no country in the world has made more progress than has Canada. Canada has organized dynamic forums on the environment and economy at both the national and provincial levels. For example, in a 1985 Canadian poll it was found that "over 94 percent of the Canadian public, believes that as individuals, they have a responsibility to prevent environmental degradation."[28]

There are some good examples in the United States of tourism development compatible with the environment. For example, the Caneel Bay Resort in St. John, U.S. Virgin Islands, is designed to accomodate tourists very comfortably without encroaching on or altering the natural surroundings. The resort has a clear policy designed to protect the environment. The policy is explained to the guests and includes guidelines for the interaction of tourists with the island's natural resources. Similarly, the 1,040-acre Ventana Canyon resort community in Arizona has been deliberately designed to be sensitive to the environment in and around the development.[29] Another resort development in Arizona, referred to as "The Boulders," is purposefully designed to blend with the surrounding area and with the natural habitat.[30] A new Hyatt Regency development near Scottsdale, Arizona, is confined to 27 areas of the 640 available acres. The remaining area is carefully maintained to protect the plant life and wildlife.[31] And in Hawaii, where many environmental mistakes were made in the Waikiki area, a clear policy has emerged to avoid such development in the future. For example the Mauna Lani Resort at Kalahuipua'a in west Hawaii took every care to enhance the environment and not obliterate it.[32] In the 1980s the technology for developing such resorts compatible with the environment evolved rapidly and it is up to the tourism policymakers and planners to make sure such technology is properly utilized in the 1990s.

CONCLUSION

There is no way to conclude a discussion about sociocultural and environmental concerns for tourism as the "book" on these issues is still "open." But it is better to bring such issues to the attention of scholars, policymakers, and planners now in order to better understand interactions and interdependence as far as tourism is concerned. It would be terrible to wake up in the year 2000 and find that conditions similar to those described in "A Parable" by Jon Rye Kinghorn in the book *New Genesis* exist:

Once upon a time there was a class
and the students expressed disapproval of their
teacher.
Why should they be concerned with
global interdependency, global problems
and what others of the world were thinking, feeling,
and doing?
And the teacher said she had a dream in which she
saw one of her students fifty years from today.
The student was angry and said,
"Why did I learn so much detail about the past
and the administration of my country
and so little about the world?"
He was angry because no one told him
that as an adult he would be faced
almost daily with problems of a
global interdependent nature, be they
problems of peace, security, quality
of life, food, inflation, or scarcity
of natural resources.
The angry student found he was the
victim as well as the beneficiary
"Why was I not warned? Why was
I not better educated? Why
did my teachers not tell me about
the problems and help me understand
I was a member of an interdependent human race?"
With even greater anger the student shouted,
"You helped me extend my hands with incredible
machines,

my eyes with telescopes and microscopes,
my brain with computers,
but you did not help me extend
my heart, love, concern
to the entire human family.
You, teacher, gave me half a loaf.[33]

Globally, the positive or negative impact of tourism on the "human family" in terms of sociocultural conditions and the environment is one of balancing the economic pressures to promote the growth of tourism with the need to consume nonrenewable resources and to properly protect the human and natural environments.

NOTES

1. A good reference on cultural development and its relationship to tourism is contained in "International Tourism Congress," a special issue of the *Journal of the Mugla School of Business Administration.*

2. *The Golden Hordes: International Tourism and the Pleasure Periphery,* by Louis Turner and John Ash, St. Martin's Press, 1976.

3. For a more complete explanation see "Cultural Richness in the U.S. Black Community Offers Great Potential for Tourism Development," by David L. Edgell and Bernetta J. Hayes, in *Business America,* September 26, 1988, pp. 8–9.

4. See "Tourism, An Economic Development Tool for Black and Minority Chambers of Commerce," by David L. Edgell, in *Business America,* February 15, 1988, p. 5.

5. This information was provided by Colonel Miguel Nieto Bastos (San Cristobal, Venezuela), one of the organizers and supporters of this event.

6. From the souvenir program of the 17th Annual Buffalo Bill Cody Days. Leavenworth, Kansas, September 20–23, 1984.

7. Reported in the *Potomac Almanac.* November 1, 1989, pp. 1, 3, and 11.

8. *Manila Declaration on World Tourism,* World Tourism Conference, Manila, the Philippines, September 27–October 10, 1980.

9. World Tourism Organization meeting of the General Assembly, Sofia, Bulgaria, September 1985.

10. For a good explanation of a potential role for the church to play in helping to develop responsible tourism, see "Tourist, Go Home!" by Kenneth D. MacHary, in *The Christian Century,* July 5–12, 1978.

11. *Tourism Management,* Salah Wahab, Tourism International Press, London, 1975.

12. For a complete explanation of the "La Ruta Maya," see the *National Geographic,* October 1989, pp. 423–505.

13. A good account of the economic and social consequences of cultural tourism in the United States is contained in "Cultural Tourism in the United States: A Learning Experience," by Anthony J. Tighe, prepared for presentation at *The First Global Conference: Tourism—A Vital Force for Peace,* Vancouver, Canada, October 23–27, 1988.

14. "Will There Be Any Nice Places Left?" Roger M. Williams, *Next,* September/October 1980, pp. 76–83.

15. Report of the *Tourism and Conservation Conference: Working Together,* European Travel Commission, London, 1974.

16. *The Washington Post,* August 3, 1985.

17. There are two excellent articles on special concerns for Venice. See *Tour and Travel News,* May 11, 1987, pp. 1 and 79, and *The Washington Post,* August 1, 1987, p. A16.

18. Many areas have fragile environments that can accommodate only a limited number of visitors. "Apocalypse in the Alps," in *Time* magazine, September 3, 1984, p. 66, discusses some of the problems of over-populated tourist destinations.

19. Tourism and immigration to the Galapagos (Ecuador) has increased to the point of almost full capacity, according to "Tourism, Immigration Put Strain on Galapagos," in *The Washington Post,* March 19, 1987, pp. A25–26.

20. "Dirty Beaches Remain Problem for the Tourism Industry," in *Caribbean Business,* November 12, 1987, presents some of the beach pollution problems in Puerto Rico.

21. From an environmentally oriented article, "Our Befouled Beaches," in *Newsweek,* July 27, 1987, p. 50.

22. This article, "Visitor Limits Planned in Some National Parks," in *The Washington Post,* June 8, 1985, p. A5, is concerned with overcrowding in certain major parks. Recently, the U.S. Park Service, U.S. Department of the Interior, has been promoting and encouraging visitors to "lesser-known parks," which often offer more interesting experiences under better conditions than can be found at the more popular parks.

23. Text of a speech by the President of India, Giani Zail Singh, inaugurating the Fifth Session of the General Assembly of the World Tourism Organization in New Delhi on October 3, 1983.

24. *U.S. News and World Report,* May 4, 1987, p. 63.

25. "Report of the United Nations Conference on the Human Environment," Stockholm, June 5–16, 1972, as reported in the "Workshop on Environmental Aspects of Tourism" organized jointly by the World Tourism

Organization and the United Nations Environmental Program, Madrid, July 5–8, 1983.

26. "Manila Declaration on World Tourism," Manila, the Philippines, October 1980 (see Appendix I).

27. The agreement was signed July 1, 1982 by the Secretary General of the World Tourism Organization and the Executive Director of the United Nations Environment Program.

28. As reported by the OECD in "Tourism and the Environment," November 25, 1988.

29. See "St. John, It's Not Just for the Rich and Famous," by June G. Naylor, in the *Fort Worth Star-Telegram,* Fort Worth, Texas, November 2, 1986. Also see "High Environmental Standards for a Desert Report," by Lew Sichelman, in *The Sunday Star-Bulletin and Advertiser,* Honolulu, Hawaii, June 9, 1985.

30. "On the Rocks," *Restaurants and Hotel Design,* July/August 1986, pp. 72–76.

31. "Resorts Catering to Nature Too," by Horace Sutton, *The Sunday Star-Bulletin and Advertiser,* Honolulu, Hawaii, December 28, 1986.

32. "Mauna Lani Resort Kalahuipua'a, West Hawaii," by Anne L. Mapes, *Hawaii Architect,* April 1987.

33. The reference to this parable was contained in *Proceedings: Governor's Tourism Congress,* December 10–11, 1984, Honolulu, Hawaii.

SUPPLEMENTAL READINGS

"Bringing Tourists to Town." Alan A. Lew. *Small Town,* July–August, 1985, pp. 4–10.

"Cultural Tourism in the USA." Anthony J. Tighe. *Tourism Management,* December 1985, pp. 234–51.

"Environmental Implications of Tourism Development." John J. Pigram. *Annals of Tourism Research,* Vol. VII No. 4, 1980, pp. 554–83.

"Environmental Planning for Tourism." Edward Inskeep. *Annals of Tourism Research,* Vol. 14, 1987, pp. 118–35.

Hosts and Guests: The Anthropology of Tourism. Valene L. Smith (ed.). Oxford: Basil Blackwell, 1978.

Preservation Forum, Vol. 2, No. 3, Fall 1988. National Trust for Historic Preservation, Washington, D.C.

The Psychology of Leisure Travel. Edward J. Mayo and Lance P. Jarvis. Boston: CBI Publishing Company, Inc., 1981.

"Scenic Oversight." Tom Arrandale. *Government Executive,* July 1988, pp. 12–17.

"Search for the Common Ground." Robert Redford. *Harvard Business Review,* Vol. 65, No. 3, May–June, 1987, p. 107.

"Sectoral Plans for Tourism Development." Luther Gordon Miller. Workshop on Environmentally Sound Tourism Development for the Caribbean Region, held at the Dover Convention Center, Bridgetown, Barbados, April 6–9, 1987.

"Tourism and the Community: A Drama in Three Acts." David A. Heenan. *Journal of Travel Research,* Spring 1978

Tourism: Economic, Physical and Social Impacts. Alister Mathieson and Geoffrey Wall. Longman Inc., New York, 1982.

Tourism Planning (2nd ed.). Clare A. Gunn. Taylor & Francis, New York, 1988.

"Tourism Planning: An Emerging Specialization." Edward Inskeep. *Journal of the American Planning Association,* Vol. 54, No. 3, Summer 1988, pp. 360–72.

"Tourism Pollution: Whose Fault Is It?" Stephan S. Halsey. *Proceedings from the Tourism and Heritage Conservation Conference,* Manila, the Philippines, November 9–11, 1981, pp. 8–10.

"Tourism's Impacts: The Social Costs to the Destination Community as Perceived by Its Residents." Abraham Pizam. *Journal of Travel Research,* Spring 1978.

"Travel Links." Sally G. Oldham. *Preservation News,* January, 1988, p. 5.

6

PROJECTIONS, IMPLICATIONS, AND POLICY PERSPECTIVES OF INTERNATIONAL TOURISM THROUGH 2000

It seems reasonable to assume that by the end of the century tourism will be one of the largest industries in the world.

Herman Kahn, The Next 200 Years, 1976.

Herman Kahn's prediction underlines the importance of planning for increased tourism in a complex and ever-changing international environment.[1] Making long-range projections is a very uncertain business.[2] Tomorrow is unknown to us, and the more tomorrows we put together, the more likely it is that events will take an unexpected turn. But, in order to properly plan and make decisions for the future growth in tourism, it is necessary to make forecasts of tourism demand. The following is an attempt to forecast worldwide tourism and international trade in tourism to the United States through the year 2000 and to suggest what the implications of such projections will be.

ASSUMPTIONS

The projections of world international tourism and international tourism to the United States through the year 2000 discussed here have been made based on some broad assumptions. These forecasts were developed assuming a relatively steady growth in the economies of the United States and of those nations of the world that are the major sources of visitors to the United States and to the world in general. It is also assumed that there will be no major natural disasters or other catastrophic effects on the tourism industry, including another major energy crisis or a continual overvaluation of the U.S. dollar, and that international impediments to travel will not increase. Finally, it is assumed that international terrorism, hijacking, and hostage-taking will not reach such proportions as to have a major detrimental impact on international travel.

BASIC FACTORS

Why make projections of international tourism in the first place? Fundamentally, the reason for such forecasting is to answer the question: "What decisions have to be made over the next ten years by businesses and governments (at all levels) to assure that tourism can grow in an orderly fashion?" In brief, planning based on future forecasts must take place now in order to assure that enough infrastructure and services will be available for a quality tourism experience in the future.

In all respects the demand for tourism is similar to the demand for most other products and services and can be explained in traditional economic terms, where the basic determinants are:

- price of the commodity
- price of competing and complementary commodities
- level of personal disposable income
- tastes, habits, and preferences of potential consumers[3]

In reality, international tourism to the United States, and to the world for that matter, is influenced by a wider number of factors, such as:

- supply of facilities
- government regulations
- disposable income levels
- introduction of new technology, particularly communication and transportation technology
- population changes
- strength (or weakness) of the U.S. dollar
- explicit and implicit barriers to travel
- health of the world economy (income and income distribution)
- level of international airfares
- promotion abroad (private and public)

- international airline and airport capacity and airline routes
- political relations with source countries
- currency devaluations
- international inflation
- availability of leisure time
- cost of accommodations, food, and entertainment

Other, less quantifiable, influences include level of education, language, customs, cultural interests, personal traits, desire for a change, business needs, shipping, mental relaxation, physical health, and spiritual well-being. The methodology utilized for the forecasts made in this chapter recognizes these factors only in the overall macro sense. Many other factors that will cause year to year changes are difficult to account for, especially for individual countries. For example, in 1992–1993, changes being made by European Community countries will impact heavily on international tourism, but it is difficult to predict what the results will be. Similarly, special events such as the Olympics, the World's Fair, and the Celebration of the five-hundredth anniversary of Columbus's discovery of America will increase tourism to Spain, but such events will impact on other countries as well. The 1994 World Cup (soccer) will be held in the United States for the first time ever and will attract large numbers of foreigners. There are many similar events that impact heavily from year to year.

METHODOLOGY

There are numerous approaches to forecasting. The two that are of prime concern in this chapter are the *theoretical* approach and the *intuitive* approach. Theoretical forecasts tend to be quantitatively oriented. Intuitive forecasting is based on empirical observations using expert opinion or judgment.

Although much research has been devoted to the development of efficient models for forecasting tourism, two major problems have been encountered by those operating in the field. First, there has been constant change in the nature and dimension of the key variables that have affected international tourism during the past few years (e.g., the rising importance of international air transport negotiations, various national currency fluctuations, and changes in the political posture towards international travel). Many of the forecasting models developed have been too static to effectively account for these kinds of variables.

The forecasts presented here use both approaches, which are mixed, modified, and further revised based on modified Delphi-type revisions.[4] Extrapolations of past data on tourism, as well as information provided by tourism experts of the World Tourism Organization, The United States Travel and Tourism Administration, private sector tourism executives, and others, were utilized to some degree to predict future international tourism. In brief, the approach taken here was simply an expert revision and adustment of time-series forecasts, modified Delphi-type insights, and considerable judgment. This approach does not presuppose a special theory, but it has been tested in one form or another in the past with some modest successes. It should be remembered that these forecasts are at the macro level and, with the exception of those for the United States, do not look at future travel flows to specific areas, although methodologies to accomplish this latter need have been developed.[5]

SOME OBSERVATIONS

Discussions with a Delphi-type panel and experts from the tourism industry about the original forecasts, which were utilized as a base for the current forecasts contained here, revealed a number of nontraditional factors. The current forecasts have included some of the earlier information as basic to the forecasts, but many revisions have been made in light of new information. The experts concluded that the purchasing power of the dollar will be a major factor in drawing increased numbers of travelers to the United States and that the movement of the dollar generally affects worldwide tourism and will continue to do so over the next ten years. The ample supply of infrastructure, the health of the world economy, new technology, less congestion, a stabilizing dollar, and improved attractions appeared to favor greater increases of tourism to the United States relative to the world in general. Hence, the growth of tourism to the United States is projected to be larger than the growth of tourism worldwide.[6] It must be recognized, however, that the dollar value is volatile and subject to dramatic shifts, as was the case in the 1980s, and therefore a shift in the forecasts is possible.

It was also felt that the United States will continue to improve its tourism facilities and infrastructure, thus making it possible for the United States to adequately handle expanded volumes of international visitors. This condition is not necessarily true worldwide, where a problem of congestion exists in some areas of the world and a lack of infrastructure will hinder others. At present, international tourism makes up about 10 percent of the total tourism revenues of the United States. This percentage could increase considerably without disrupting the orderly growth of tourism in the United States. There is currently ample shoulder-season carrying capacity and a wide variety of year-round tourism destinations to successfully accommodate increased numbers of foreign visitors. In addition, the experts suggest that many new tourism attractions will be developed in the U.S. over the next decade. The pool of experts therefore have concluded that the U.S. could receive an increased volume of foreign visitors for many years into the future without putting undue stress on the infrastructure or causing environmental damage, if decisions and plans for future growth are made now.

Some areas of the world will see shortages of infrastructure and facilities. For example, over the next few years, there will likely be an increased demand for tourism to Eastern Europe; yet the available infrastructure and facilities in Eastern Europe are not yet adequate to handle large amounts of increased tourism. The same situation appears to be true in the popular cities in the Soviet Union. The challenge for these areas and others around the world will only be met by careful planning and the implementation of clear growth policies.

It is possible that the expansion of tourism to the United States will have to contend with major improvements in general transportation policy (more about this later). Airport congestion, higher energy costs or inadequate fuel supplies, and problems relating to the granting or continuance of international air routes may pose problems for international tourism growth in the next decade. However, the tourism experts suggest that the air transport problems can be resolved with more effective route operation, improved airport facilities, and the development of more efficient aircraft. Also, recent forecasts by the U.S. Department of Energy have indicated that adequate supplies of fuel will be available during the next decade, but possibly at increased cost.

RESULTS

Worldwide visitor arrivals and tourism receipts will increase substantially over the next ten years. Tourism arrivals were approximately 400 million in 1989; in the year 2000 it is estimated that arrivals will be over 500 million (see Table 6.1). Global tourism receipts were over $200 billion in 1989. In the year 2000, this figure will likely be

TABLE 6.1
Foreign Visitor Arrivals and Travel Receipts 1960–2000

Year	World Int'l Tourism Arrivals (millions)	Foreign Visitor Arrivals to the U.S. (millions)	U.S. Share (%)	World Int'l Tourism Receipts ($ billions)*	U.S. Travel Receipts ($ billions)*	U.S. Share (%)
1960	69	5.6	8	$ 6.9	1.02	15
1965	113	7.8	7	11.6	1.54	13
1970	160	12.4	8	17.9	2.70	15
1971	172	12.7	7	20.9	2.95	14
1972	182	13.1	7	24.6	2.82	11
1973	191	14.0	7	31.1	3.41	11
1974	197	14.2	7	33.8	4.03	12
1975	214	15.7	7	40.7	4.70	12
1976	221	17.5	8	44.4	5.74	13
1977	239	18.5	8	55.6	6.15	11
1978	257	19.7	8	68.8	7.19	10
1979	274	20.3	7	83.3	8.44	10
1980	285	22.3	8	102.4	10.59	10
1981	289	23.5	8	104.3	12.91	12
1982	287	21.8	8	98.6	12.39	13
1983	284	21.7	8	98.5	11.41	12
1984(R)	312	26.9	9	109.6	17.75	16
1985(R)	326	25.7	8	114.8	17.93	16
1986(R)	334	26.3	8	138.5	20.45	15
1987(R)	360	29.7	8	169.4	23.51	14
1988(R)	391	34.2	9	193.4	29.20	15
1989(P)	403	38.3	10	208.7	34.31	16
1990(P)	412	40.7	10	225.0	38.74	17
1995(P)	472	52.5	11	263.2†	50.10†	19
2000(P)	532	67.0	13	304.3†	63.90†	21

SOURCE: World Tourism Organization and U.S. Department of Commerce (United States Travel and Tourism Administration and Bureau of Economic Analysis)
*Excludes international passenger fare payments
†Expressed in 1990 (constant) dollars
(P) Projected
(R) Revised data series; not comparable with previous years

over $300 billion expressed in 1990 (constant) dollars. Table 6.1 illustrates the past, present, and future for worldwide tourism.

Forecasted U.S. foreign visitor arrivals by the year 2000 will approach 67 million and receipts will approximate $64 billion in 1990 dollars, as shown in Table 6.1. These forecasts are based on past tourism trends, expert opinions, considerable judgment, and other factors and are not intended to favor one or more rigid sets of theoretical statistical methodologies.

The actual numbers are not so important, but the direction of the trends is significant. For both arrivals and receipts the direction of the growth is considerable for both the world and the United States. The rate of growth for the United States is higher than that for the world, which certainly follows recent trends and which supports the assumptions and factors cited above. In both cases, the tourism growth trends are quite different from previous periods in terms of magnitude. The important point is that there will be substantial growth in worldwide tourism over the next ten years. International tourism will likely be growing more rapidly than the world's gross national product, and tourism will become increasingly more important in the global economy. The implications for such growth are critical for the decision-making process in the public and private sector.

IMPLICATIONS OF PROJECTIONS

A principal reason for making tourism forecasts in the first place is so that the decision makers who are responsible for the development and implementation of public policy programs and private sector initiative have some parameters or guidelines for making decisions. Armed with such information, the public policy official and private sector executive can assess the impact that tourism has on the entire economy, lifestyles, national resources, profit potentials, investment decisions, domestic and foreign relations, and balance of payments.[7] There are wide implications, which stem from the expected developments in tourism in the next ten years. Some of the more obvious ones are identified at this time and are mentioned in the following paragraphs.

Worldwide tourism may be reaching the point that, in terms of economic development, Walt Rostow called the "takeoff" into sustained growth, such that by the year 2000 we may reach a period of mass consumption of tourism.[8] This trend should be strongly supported by the anticipated relative decrease in the cost of transportation (in comparison with costs of other goods and/or services) as we see larger and faster aircraft come into existence. There will also be worldwide increases in per capita income, thus giving larger numbers of people the economic means to travel.

In the year 2000 the real income per person throughout the world will be much higher than it is today. In addition, the graying population, the major group with higher levels of income and leisure time, will be growing rapidly. Women, another major segment of the population, now possess a larger share of disposable income and are traveling more. As a result there will be a much larger amount of discretionary income available for activities such as pleasure travel. In the future, this discretionary income will be spread more widely across the income pyramid, resulting in a larger proportion of the world's population traveling than travels today. International tourists will include more individuals from the lower end of the income distribution as well as those from the upper end who form the bulk of today's travelers.

Assuming that aircraft technology increases productivity and that no unusual increases in the cost of jet fuel take place, the relative cost of air transportation will continue to decline over the next ten years. A decline in the relative price of transportation is important because the growth sector of air travel is in pleasure travel (according to the World Tourism Organization, "holiday travel" is double "business travel"), which is more price-sensitive than time-sensitive. Price is of paramount importance, and scheduling is less important because pleasure travel plans generally are made with considerable advance planning.[9] As a consequence of an increase in income and a relative decrease in transportation costs, pleasure travel will continue to increase.

As a result of much more widespread international tourism, there will be greater international personal contact and knowledge about the rest of the world. There will be greater cosmopolitanism and less provincialism in the sense that traveling widely will be the expectation of greater numbers of people, and little of the world will be totally unknown or unfamiliar. There will be no "dark continents" because travel will shed light on the darkness. There will be a much greater possibility for creating a world of international understanding.

The economic impact of international tourism will be greater than it is today. International tourism will become a more important part of the world economy as tourism grows more rapidly than other areas of the economy do. There will be several results. A larger portion of jobs and income will derive directly from international tourism. The impact on the balance of payments will be greater. Particularly for the United States, this will mean that a growing proportion of U.S. export earnings will come from selling tourism services (to foreign tourists) rather than from exporting merchandise. And selected state and local economies will be heavily supported by international tourism.

The role of international politics will have a greater impact on the international tourism sector. Tourism may become even more sensitive to the policies of governments as it grows in size. Impediments to travel such as the control of visas and passports, travel allowance restrictions, and foreign exchange will have the ability to stymie travel. Alternatively, elimination or amelioration of these impediments will have the power to facilitate tourism. More nations are likely to have bilateral trade negotiations that include agreements to mutually reduce the impediments to travel.

Environmental issues will become increasingly important. As the numbers of tourists increase, the problems of "crowding" in tourist areas will become more acute, especially in areas that are limited spatially or in their ability to absorb large numbers of people. Fragile natural environments such as the Alaskan frozen tundra or the Rocky Mountain soil above the timberline can be trampled and destroyed by tourist hordes. Museums and public buildings can quickly become overcrowded. There will be a greater need to plan for tourist growth to ease crowding and prevent damage to the natural environment. One step in this direction is to reduce the seasonality of tourism.[10]

A related problem is the absorptive capacity of an economy with respect to tourism. This questions the ability of an area to supply enough tourist infrastructure and facilities to handle the demand of tourists. There can be limitations because of labor shortages, capital shortages, land shortages, and so on. These shortages may be due to natural scarcity or because of alternative demands on the resources available. Also, the local population may find alternative uses of resources preferable to setting them aside for tourism. Such resistance to using resources to increase absorptive capacity relative to tourism could become particularly important if local opposition to tourism increases because of environmental or sociocultural concerns.

As tourism increases, so will demands on other sectors of the economy. For example, more airplanes, cruise ships, and automobiles will need to be manufactured. Construction of hotels, restaurants, and attractions will take place. Agricultural products will be in greater demand. The list goes on and on, but the outcome should be one of positive economic impact in a broad spectrum of the economy.

Technology will continue to impact heavily on the travel industry. For example, research is underway to develop an aerospace plane that could fly from the United States to Japan in about two hours and take off and land at conventional airports. Many other changes in the manufacture of aircraft are taking place. This, in turn, will mean restructuring and changing or building some new airport facilities. Information technology will continue to produce changes in the travel trade.

The Immigration Reform and Control Act of 1986 in the United States provides for a "Visa Waiver Pilot Program for Certain Visitors." Under this section of the Act, the Attorney General and the Secretary of State are authorized to establish a pilot program to waive the visa requirements for up to eight countries that qualify under the law. If the countries selected under this provision continue in the same positive vein as is currently indicated, then there will be pressure to make the visa waiver program permanent. If the program is expanded at a later time, the potential for future growth in international tourism to the United States would be even more substantial than is forecasted.

When the trade ministers of the world agreed at the GATT talks in September 1986 to include "negotiations on trade in services," they opened up potential opportunities for reducing barriers to international travel as well. If substantial progress is made to add tourism as one of the sectors for inclusion in the negotiations on trade in services, then international tourism would have the potential to grow even more rapidly.

POLICY PERSPECTIVES

The 1990s may very well be recorded in future years as the most important decade for formulating policies on tourism. As the preceding chapters suggest, and as the forecasts in this chapter imply, the tourism industry will be faced with some difficult challenges over the next several years. Private sector managers and public sector executives charged with making present and future decisions on tourism issues will need a managerial framework for analyzing the various alternatives so that a course of action can be selected.[11]

The leaders, executives, and planners in the tourism industry have begun to realize the need for a greater focus on policy. There is a need for greater articulation of tourism policy goals and objectives arrived at through deliberate and conscientious discussion. The problems of tourism are known, the importance of tourism is known, and now it is time to present guidelines for tourism policy formulation, no matter how loosely structured.[12]

Fundamentally, whether it be at the local, regional, national, or international level, it is policy that determines the goals and objectives and provides the guidelines for tourism development. The policy issues may differ for developing as opposed to developed countries, or the stage of tourism formulation may differ, but ultimately it is policy that drives the other aspects of tourism, whether it be on the demand or on the supply side. Tourism policy must be dynamic in the sense that the changing environment (political, social, or economic) must be adjusted to as the policies are formulated and implemented.

Many influences may cause a policy to shift in one direction or another. These may take the form of government policy at the city, state (or other territorial division, depending on the country), or federal level. In some countries, private sector influences shape national tourism policy. In addition, most countries have laws and regulations that influence policy decisions on tourism. Also of importance are the influences exerted by international tourism organizations.

ASPECTS OF U.S. GOVERNMENT TOURISM POLICY

Government involvement in tourism will vary from country to country. In many countries, the production of travel and tourism services is in fact both regulated and operated by the government. The United States is used here as just an example of national tourism policy.

The United States Travel and Tourism Administration (USTTA) was established in 1981 in the U.S. Department of Commerce by the National Tourism Policy Act (NTPA). It replaced the United States Travel Service, which was created by the International Travel Act of 1961. The NTPA empowers the Secretary of Commerce to:

- develop, plan, and carry out a comprehensive program to stimulate travel to the United States by residents of foreign countries

- encourage the development of tourist facilities, package tours, and other arrangements within the United States for meeting the requirements of foreign visitors

- foster and encourage the widest possible distribution of the benefits of travel between foreign countries and the United States, consistent with sound economic principles

- encourage the simplification, reduction, or elimination of barriers to travel and the facilitation of international travel generally

- collect, publish, and provide for the exchange of statistics and technical information, including schedules of meetings, fairs, and other attractions relating to international travel and tourism

- establish facilitation services at major U.S. ports of entry

- consult with foreign governments on travel and tourism matters and . . . represent U.S. tourism interests before international and intergovernmental meetings

- develop and administer a comprehensive program relating to travel industry information, data service, training and education, and technical assistance

- develop a program to seek and receive information on a continuing basis from the tourism industry, including consumer and travel trade associations, regarding needs and interests that should be met by a Federal agency or program and to direct that information to the appropriate agency or program

- encourage to the maximum extent feasible travel to and from the United States on U.S. carriers

- assure coordination within the Department of Commerce so that, to the extent practicable, all the resources of the Department are used to effectively and efficiently carry out the national tourism policy

- develop and submit annually to the Congress, within six weeks of transmittal to the Congress of the President's recommended budget . . . a detailed marketing plan to stimulate and encourage travel to the United States during the fiscal year for which such budget is submitted.

Tourism Policy Council

The NTPA also created an interagency Tourism Policy Council (TPC). The TPC brings together high-level agency officials with direct program operating responsibilities to consult and discuss needed improvements, to examine specific tourism-related programs, and to assist in resolving interagency conflicts should such arise. Because it is chaired by the Secretary of Commerce, the TPC raises tourism coordination to the highest level of authority. The Under Secretary of Commerce for Travel and Tourism serves as vice chairperson in the absence of the Secretary.

The TPC is comprised of representatives from the Office of Management and Budget, the Commerce Department's International Trade Administration, and the Departments of Transportation, the Interior, State, Labor, and Energy. The chairperson may invite representatives of nonmember agencies to participate in the functions of the TPC. The Act explicitly establishes membership on the TPC at the cabinet and subcabinet level, with allowance for designation of alternate representation by an individual with decision-making authority. The United States Travel and Tourism Administration (USTTA) of the Department of Commerce is responsible for coordinating and organizing the meetings of the TPC. The TPC, as specified by the Act, has four main functions:

- Coordinate the policies and programs of federal agencies that have a significant effect on tourism, recreation, and national heritage preservation

- Develop areas of cooperative program activity

- Assist in resolving interagency policy and program conflicts

- Seek and receive concerns and views of state and local governments as well as the travel industry relative to federal policies and programs deemed to conflict with the orderly growth and development of tourism

Since the first meeting of the TPC in January 1982, the TPC has set up staff-level working groups to focus on particular policy areas, reviewed numerous federal programs related to tourism, facilitated interagency cooperation and coordination, sought to identify and seek solutions to interagency and intergovernmental tourism-related problems, and initiated a process for exchanging tourism information among agencies.

The Tourism Policy Council epitomizes the intent and significance of the National Tourism Policy Act of 1981. It has caused diverse segments of the government that sometimes worked at cross purposes in tourism matters prior to the establishment of the TPC to cooperate and coordinate their respective policies which impact on tourism. U.S. tourism policy in the future will demand far greater coordination between government agencies, the private sector, and state and local entities; as a result, the TPC will play an even more important role in the country's tourism policies.

Travel and Tourism Advisory Board

The NTPA established an additional policy in the form of a Travel and Tourism Advisory Board. A difficulty in developing and establishing any kind of board is to determine its size, its representation, and its political composition. If a board becomes too large, it becomes unwieldy and unmanageable. One research source, which analyzed organizational structures, suggests (depending on the board's purposes) that the most effective and efficient board structures have membership levels somewhere between eight and fifteen members. Fewer than eight does not seem to provide the diversity and wide range of experience needed for an effective board, and more than fifteen seems to encumber the efficiency and management of the board. The NTPA provides for a board with fifteen members appointed by the Secretary of Commerce.

An additional problem in the United States for governmental boards is to overcome the potential political affiliation biases of the board members. If too many members belong to a single political party the potential exists for politically motivated decisions by the board. To alleviate this potential problem, the Act specifies that "not more than eight members of the Board shall be appointed from the same political party."

Another key question is the representativeness of the board. If the appointing authority is not careful, there will be an unbalanced representation from certain segments of the tourism industry or from narrowly defined geographical regions. To help avoid this problem, the Act provides that "as nearly as practicable a broad representation of different geographical regions within the United States and of the diverse and varied segments of the tourism industry" will be represented on the Board. It further provides that "the members shall be appointed from senior executive officers" (or chief executive officers) from the travel and tourism industry. The Act also specifies that at least one board member must be *a.* a senior representative from a labor organization representing employees of the tourism industry; *b.* a representative of the states who is knowledgeable of tourism promotion; *c.* a consumer advocate or ombudsman from the organized public interest community; *d.* an economist, statistician, or accountant; and *e.* an individual from the academic community who is knowledgeable in tourism, recreation, or national heritage conservation. The remaining members of the fifteen-member board must demonstrate broad representation of the tourism community.

To ensure continuity on the board, the Act provides that members be appointed for a term of office of three years, except that of the members first appointed, "(1) four members shall be appointed for terms of one year, and (2) four members shall be appointed for terms of two years" and "no members of the Board shall be eligible to serve in excess of two consecutive terms of three years each."

Two of the key responsibilities of the board include advising the Secretary of Commerce on implementation of the National Tourism Policy Act of 1981 and advising the Assistant Secretary for Tourism Marketing with respect to the preparation of the United States Travel and Tourism Administration's (USTTA) annual marketing plan. This latter responsibility is particularly important to USTTA because the agency, by law, must "submit annually to the Congress . . . a detailed marketing plan to stimulate and encourage travel to the United

States. . . ." The Membership of the board, as described above, is uniquely qualified to perform both of these tasks.

In brief, then, the board is a vital part of the tourism policy process in the United States. It reviews governmental tourism programs and recommends those which should receive high-priority treatment. It seeks to assure that tourism will receive its rightful place as an integral part of overall policies and plans for future governmental programs.

Tourism Policy Decision-Making Process[13]

Very little has been written about the process for making policy decisions in tourism. For most countries, the policy decisions regarding tourism have focused on only two goals: maximizing tourist arrivals and improving the balance of payments through international tourism receipts.

One attempt to focus attention on the need for systematic planning for policy decisions in tourism took place during the joint national meeting of the Operations Research Society–The Institute of Management Sciences, Miami Beach, Florida, November 3–6, 1976. In a paper, "Public Policy Planning and Operations Research in the Tourism Sector: Never the Twain Shall Meet—Or Shall They?" by Edgell et al. (1976), a conceptual representation of the current policy process was presented (Fig. 6.1), and in this same paper, a system model was presented (see Fig. 6.2).

It is necessary to recognize that on any given tourism issue, the policymaker does not make a decision in a vacuum nor always in the same way. The policymaker almost always has certain goals and

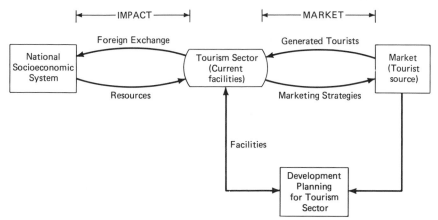

Figure 6.1. Conceptual representation of current process.

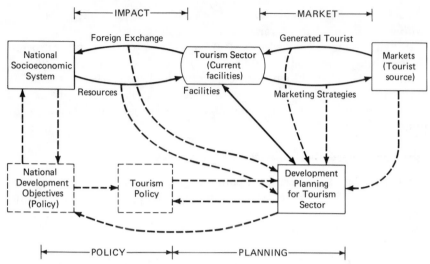

Figure 6.2. Conceptual representation of the system model of the tourism sector.

objectives as a guide in the decision-making process. These also vary considerably from country to country. At the same time, numerous other considerations must be accounted for. This is presented visually in Figure 6.3.

Another way of looking at the decision-making process is through

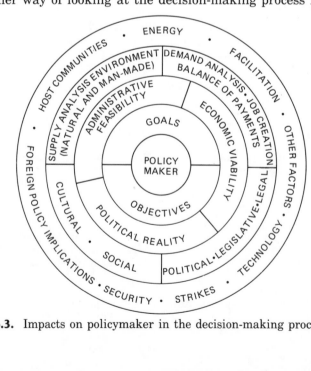

Figure 6.3. Impacts on policymaker in the decision-making process.

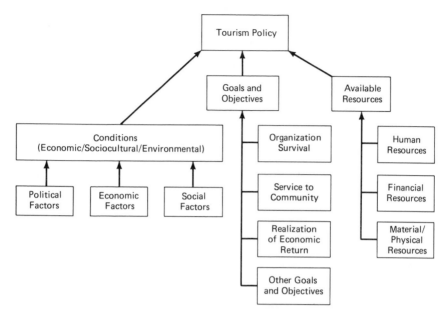

Figure 6.4. The tourism policy development/decision process. Basic tourism policy equation: $P = f(G) + f(R) + f(E)$, where P = the tourism policy developed; G = the goals and objectives; R = the resources available; E = the given conditions.

the use of an equation. Figure 6.4 shows a basic simple equation that summarizes another approach in tourism policy decision making.

Based on numerous observations and experience, a good description of the process can be shown in Figure 6.5. This general approach looks at each tourism issue separately. It suggests that tourism issues reflect not only economic considerations but sociocultural and environmental concerns as well, and it points out some of the principal influences on the decision process, some of which were outlined earlier in this book.

NOTES

1. It should be noted that the idea that tourism will likely be one of the largest industries by the year 2000 was not necessarily developed first by Herman Kahn, although he certainly was the most famous futurist to do so. On September 13, 1964, at the Opening Convention Session of the National Association of Travel Organizations in New York, Charles Gillett, as President of the National Association of Travel Organizations, had this to say: "I believe that the increases in leisure that are being created by automation will give us such tremendous opportunities

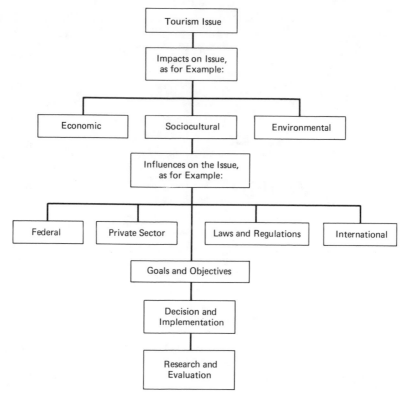

Figure 6.5. International tourism policy formulation: general diagram.

that the travel industry may well become the world's largest industry within the next 25 years."

2. For an interesting commentary with forecasts, see "International Business Prospects for the Rest of the Century: International Tourism and Travel," by David L. Edgell, in *Travel Research Journal,* Edition 1977, World Tourism Organization, Madrid, Spain.

3. A good detailed discussion of tourism forecasting is contained in Brian Archer's book, *Demand Forecasting in Tourism,* University of Wales Press, Bangor, Wales, 1976. See also "An Overview of Approaches Used to Forecast Tourism Demand," by Muzaffer Uysal and John L. Crompton, in *Journal of Travel Research.*

4. "Forecasts of International Tourism to the U.S.A.," by David L. Edgell, Richard L. Seely, and Harvey J. Iglarsh, in the *International Journal of Tourism Management,* June 1980, pp. 109–13.

5. For an introduction to tourism forecasting for regions and states, see "A Multi-stage Model for the Development of International Tourism Forecasts for States and Regions," by David L. Edgell and Richard L. Seely,

in Tourism Planning and Development Issues, George Washington University, Washington, D.C. 1980. See also "Use of Modified Scenarios Research in Forecasting of Tourism in the United States," in the *Travel Research Journal,* Madrid, Spain, 1979, pp. 49–57. In addition, Anthony Edwards, writing in the *International Tourism Quarterly* over the years, has refined methodologies for forecasting to individual countries.

6. For information regarding the forecasts that are the basis for the forecasts in this chapter, see *International Tourism Prospects 1987–2000,* by David L. Edgell, U.S. Department of Commerce, Washington, D.C., February 1987, pp. 29–34. See also "Forecasts of International Tourism to the U.S.A." by David L. Edgell, Richard L. Seely, and Harvey J. Iglarsh, in *International Journal of Tourism Management,* June 1980, pp. 109–13.

7. This point is discussed in "Use of Modified Scenario Research in Forecasting of Tourism in the United States," by George Tesar, David L. Edgell, and Richard L. Seely, in *Travel Research Journal,* Edition 1979/1, World Tourism Organization, Madrid, Spain.

8. *The Stages of Economic Growth,* by Walt W. Rostow, Cambridge University Press, Cambridge and New York, 1960.

9. "Air Transport and Tourism," in the *1976 International Economics Report of the President,* Washington, D.C., January 1977, Chapter 10.

10. Attempts to reduce the seasonality in tourism are already underway in Europe. For a discussion of German efforts in this area, see the Organization for Economic Cooperation and Development, Tourism Committee, "Staggering Holidays" (mimeographed), Paris, January 1977.

11. "The Formulation of Tourism Policy—A Managerial Framework" (Chapter 3), by David L. Edgell, in *Travel, Tourism, and Hospitality Research,* ed. by J. R. Brent Ritchie and Charles R. Goeldner, New York: John Wiley and Sons, 1987, pp. 23–33. This presentation addresses some of the key policy issues and influences on tourism policy and also presents an introductory explanation of the formulation of tourism policy as a tool to aid in policy decision making.

12. Clare A. Gunn discusses the importance of tourism planning and policy and that so often the orientation in tourism is toward the demand side with little interest in the supply side. For a good discussion of some of the basic principles important to planning and policy, see *Tourism Planning,* by Clare A. Gunn, New York: Taylor and Francis, 1988, pp. 269–83.

13. Much of the material in this section is taken directly from the chapter cited in Note 11. This information and the charts were developed over a period of years as part of the author's notes as adjunct professor at the George Washington University and as a special professor at the Executive Development Institute for Tourism at the University of Hawaii.

SUPPLEMENTAL READINGS

The Delphi Method: Techniques and Applications. Harold A. Linstone and Murray Turoff. Reading, Mass.: Addison-Wesley Publishing Company, 1975.

Demand Forecasting in Tourism. Brian Archer. Cardiff: University of Wales Press, 1976.

Economic Forecasting. Herman O. Stekler. New York: Praeger Publishers, 1970.

"Forecasting Tourism, Revisited." Dexter J. L. Choy. *Tourism Management,* September 1984, pp. 171–76.

"Hawaii Tourism to the Year 2000: A Delphi Forecast." Juanita C. Liu. *Tourism Management,* December 1988, pp. 279–90.

"International Tourism Forecasts to 1995." Anthony Edwards. *International Tourism Quarterly,* Special Report No. 53, 1985, pp. 52–64.

"A Model of Tourism Flow into the Pacific." L. J. Crampton and K. T. Tan. *Revue du Tourisme,* July-September 1973, pp. 98–104.

"An Overview of Approaches Used to Forecast Tourism Demand." Muzaffer Uysal and John L. Crompton. *Journal of Travel Research,* Spring, 1985, pp. 7–15.

Planning for Tourism Development: Quantitative Approaches. Charles Gearing, William Swart, and Turgut Var. New York: Praeger Publishers, 1976.

"Programming Tomorrow's Tourists." Michael W. Duttweiler and Michael Voiland. *Extensive Review,* Winter, 1984, pp. 17–19.

Public Policy Planning and Operations Research in the Tourism Sector. David L. Edgell, Charles Gearing, Rodney Stiefbold, and William Swart. Paper presented at the Joint National Meeting of the Operations Research Society–The Institute of Management Sciences, Miami Beach, Florida, November 3–6, 1976.

"The Role of Government in Promoting Tourism." David L. Edgell. *Business America,* May 28, 1984.

Thriving on Chaos. Tom Peters. New York: Harper and Row, 1987.

Tourism Analysis. Stephen L. J. Smith. John Wiley and Sons, Inc., New York, 1989.

"Tourism Forecasting: A Review of Empirical Research." Pauline Sheldon and Turgut Var. *Journal of Forecasting,* Vol. 4, No. 2, pp. 7–15.

Tourism Planning. Clare A. Gunn. New York: Taylor and Francis, 1988.

Tourism Policy Formulation Through Management Science. David L. Edgell, Charles Gearing, Rodney Stiefbold, and William Swart. Paper presented at the XXIII International Meeting of the Institute of Management Sciences, Athens, Greece, July 25–27, 1977.

The Travel Safety Handbook. Alan T. Stutts. New York: Van Nostrand Reinhold, 1990.

Travel, Tourism, and Hospitality Research. J. R. Brent Ritchie and Charles R. Goeldner (eds.). New York: John Wiley and Sons, 1987.

7

FUTURE POLICY ISSUES IN TOURISM

It is hardly possible to overrate the value, in the present low state of human improvement, of placing human beings in contact with persons dissimilar to themselves and with modes of thought and action unlike those with which they are familar.

John Stuart Mill, Principles of Political Economy, 1848.

The prior chapters point toward a bright future for worldwide tourism. This does not mean that there are not problems—the tourism industry is fraught with enormous difficulties. I believe, however, that through tourism policy, awareness, and education, the general public and key policymakers will begin to realize just how significant tourism is to the economic strength and social vitality of most nations of the world. All countries of the world share in the burdens and benefits of tourism and need to work cooperatively toward a higher-quality tourism product worldwide. The tourism product in this context means the total tourism experience in terms of not only the destination, but also facilitation, transportation, security and safety, and other features pertinent to a quality tourism experience. I also feel that well-conceived tourism policies will benefit the consumer, government, the private sector, and the world community at large and will be a major factor in improving every aspect of the tourism product.

One way to assist in the international tourism policy dialogue is to outline some of the issues that will confront policymakers over the next decade. The following paragraphs will briefly introduce a few of the key issues that I have identified as important in opening the door to a higher quality tourism experience for the world in the twenty-first century. While much of the focus in this identification process is through the tourism "eyes" of the United States, almost all countries of the world will face the same kinds of questions at one point or another in the future development of their tourism product.

TRANSPORTATION AND COMMUNICATION
IMPACTS ON TOURISM

As was mentioned at the beginning of this book, transportation and communication technology have been at the forefront of progress in worldwide tourism. The future will be no different; these two factors are integral to all tourism policy initiatives developed over the next decade. They cannot be treated adequately here because transportation and communication policy are complete disciplines in their own right. But I would be remiss, indeed, if I failed to at least briefly acknowledge their interrelationship with tourism.

Some basic issues with respect to transportation that will impact on the future of tourism include:

- addressing concerns with respect to transportation accidents and fatalities

- addressing terrorism issues in general, but particularly in transportation

- addressing the continued problems of congestion, especially on highways, in the skies, and at airports

- addressing a broad spectrum of concerns on pollution

- addressing a wide range of aviation issues through air transport negotiations

- addressing new concerns resulting from changes in transportation technology such as high-speed "bullet" trains or hypersonic airplanes sometimes referred to as "scram-jets"

- addressing questions of expansion of airports, runways, and air traffic control systems

- addressing issues such as providing essential transportation services to small cities and rural communities

- addressing city concerns for increased air access to more international destinations

These are just a few of the transportation issues that need to be addressed as far as the future of tourism is concerned. But then, tourism has been adjusting to transportation technology for centuries. Over the years there have been changes from foot travel to the horse and camel, to the chariot, to steam-powered ships and trains, to the automobile, to the various stages of airplane development, and now to the space shuttle. The difference is that adjustments today must take place in a shorter time-span and must take place at the same time that other dynamic changes are impacting on society.

Communications technology likewise has revolutionized the travel and tourism industry. There are now communication networks that link clients, tourism operators, and suppliers of tourism services throughout the world. And for much of the travel world, computerese has become a second language. Furthermore, videos are emerging in every facet of the travel industry, not only in terms of destination planning, marketing, and promotion but as agents for change in information and education about tourism.

In addition, today we have fax machines, elaborate touristic data banks, sophisticated airline reservation systems, computerized accommodations booking facilities, special uses of credit cards, and direct dialing to practically every part of the world. These are only a few of the examples of changes in communication technology that impact on tourism. Almost every aspect of the tourism industry has been affected by the installation of new communications and information technology systems.

Certainly, technology in transportation and communication has revolutinized tourism, and, for the most part, the industry has responded with enthusiasm. Moreover, many questions unrelated to technological change in transportation and communication are posing interesting dilemmas for the tourism industry. The question for policymakers is whether the tourism industry is ready to adjust to even more dramatic changes in transportation and communication technology in the 1990s.

ENTERING THE INTERNATIONAL MARKETPLACE

Not unrelated to the prior item is the need for more recognition at the policy level by states, territories, and the private sector of the advantages of conducting their tourism business in the international marketplace. Most tourism entities in the United States have pursued policy initiatives oriented toward the domestic tourism market because it is larger, more familiar, easier to enter, has lower operating costs, and has fewer barriers to overcome. Furthermore, because much of the tourism industry in the United States is composed of small firms, it is often difficult to understand and access the international marketing intelligence and data or to find out where to go for technical assistance. Some progress has been made in overcoming some of these shortcomings through cooperative marketing efforts, regionally designed programs, and individual state and industry initiatives. But the surface has only been scratched; other opportunities exist and must be recognized and utilized.

Often, unfortunately, too much of the attention by governments, both national and local, has focused on the more glamorous marketing and promotion of inbound tourist business rather than on policy approaches that deal with reduction or removal of restrictions to tourism on a worldwide basis and facilitate the entry and operation of tourism business worldwide. The United States already has a comparative advantage in marketing its tourism destinations, and the U.S. private sector conducts excellent promotion and marketing campaigns. Where the United States has a competitive disadvantage in the international marketplace is in obtaining a fair and equal opportunity to pursue its tourism products in an unrestricted marketplace. If most of the barriers and obstacles to international tourism were removed or reduced tomorrow, the United States and other countries of the world could compete for an ever larger tourism market than currently exists and worldwide tourism would be greatly expanded. An unrestricted international marketplace would encourage and facilitate easy entry for small (and large) businesses, states, and local entities and thus assist in the overall strategy to increase the number of businesses marketing their tourism products abroad. Developing such strategies in the 1990s will be a real tourism policy challenge.

SEASONALITY IN TOURISM

One area that a national, state, or local tourism policy must address is the matter of seasonality of tourism demand. Seasonality in tourism causes underemployment, underutilization of facilities, and in turn, a lowered productivity. Unlike merchandise, which can, be stored in inventory until it is sold, the "wares" of the travel industry have no "shelf-life." Hotel room-nights, airline, train and motorcoach seat-miles, car rental-hours, and restaurant table-space are perishable; they cannot be returned to supply if they go unused, and they earn no "rent" for whatever period they are unconsumed. The seasonality problem is worsened because most people want to take their vacations during the third quarter, when most schools observe summer vacation.

Some countries of Europe have implemented year-round school policies or school vacation schedules staggered by province. The impetus for this policy arose more than a decade ago when, on the first day after schools had let out for the summer in Holland, Belgium, and West Germany, there was a traffic jam on West German highways that lasted *three days!* If the United States does not begin thinking about innovative solutions to the seasonality problem now, there could be serious difficulties in the future. Some progress has been made. For example, several states have delayed the start of the school year until after Labor Day, and many others are considering this move. This both lengthens the tourist "season" and makes available student workers needed in camps and resort areas. Some cities have turned to year-round school systems to avoid crowded conditions in the classroom. This leads to staggered vacations, which have a positive impact on the travel industry. Positive policies to resolve the seasonality problems are needed in more countries, states/provinces, and cities.

THE ENVIRONMENT AND TOURISM

Increasingly educated travelers actively seek unspoiled environments as holiday destinations. This raises the challenge of meeting rising expectations as far as tourism and the environment are concerned. We often speak of tourism as a renewable economic resourse. But that economic resource depends on a healthy environment. Take away the environment and you lose the renewable resource.

Already many areas of the world suffer from pollution and a deterioration of the environment. There are beautiful and scenic mountain areas where slashes into the forest to meet the demand for ski slopes offer the potential for avalanches in the winter and mud slides in the summer. Mountain trails are littered with beer and soft-drink cans and other debris. One only need visit certain beaches to understand the crowding and pollution problems along the coastlines of the world. Some beachfront hotels are so numerous as to spoil the scenic view of the beach that attracted tourists in the first place. Other tourism areas are overcrowded, noisy, tastelessly developed, and environmentally polluted.

In 1989, for example, the world followed the tragic disaster of the Exxon Valdez oil spill in Alaska, which wreaked havoc on tourism to Alaska. Had this catastrophe occurred, for instance, in Basel, Switzerland, on the Rhine River, the devastation of the environment would have reached the whole length of the river—through all of Germany and the Netherlands to Rotterdam and on across the channel to the Dover coast. You could have forgotten about romantic cruises on the Rhine for years and years to come. This world cannot afford many Valdez-type disasters or Chernobyl-type accidents.

Recently, considerable progress has been made in resolving some of these problems. Some real-estate developers, for example, have been innovative and creative in tending to the needs of the tourist while at the same time seeking to maintain or improve the environment. A visit to Baltimore's Inner Harborplace, Boston's Faneuil Hall and Marketplace, Charleston and Savannah's historic preservation areas, Old San Juan, or similar destinations attests to the fact that tourism development interests can go hand in hand with the environment. With the likelihood that tourism will grow over the next ten years, it would behoove the tourism industry to develop innovative tourism development policies that will accommodate the tourist and at the same time preserve the natural environment.

EDUCATION AND TRAINING

Educational and training programs emerge almost daily in response to the growth of the tourism industry. In the ultimate analysis, the success of the travel and tourism industry in the global environment will depend on its degree of professionalism. Tourism education and training programs will need to be strengthened if a more professional tourism work force is to emerge. In question is the quality and direction of such programs.

Many programs exist for quality training of unskilled and semi-skilled workers, if the employer knows where to go or who to ask about such programs. Programs beyond the vocational training level are more limited. One of the best-designed short-term programs to improve managerial and leadership skills is offered at the Executive Development Institute for Tourism, housed at the University of Hawaii. This program does an excellent job in serving the ongoing educational needs of executives and professionals in private and public sectors of international tourism. Another excellent short-term program—designed to provide additional training to managers, supervisory personnel, and management trainees from the hospitality, retailing, and tourism industries—is the series of management seminars on hospitality, retailing, and tourism that has been conducted at the University of the U.S. Virgin Islands. In addition, many U.S. universities now have undergraduate and graduate degree programs in tourism and hotel management for students interested in career development in tourism.

One problem with academic education in tourism has been the lack of good tourism textbooks or other publications appropriate as teaching tools for tourism courses. Fortunately, over the past five years more texts of a higher quality have been written about tourism subjects than were written in the previous twenty-five years. Another weak area in tourism education and training yet to be resolved is the lack of tourism education or awareness programs at the grade school and high school level.

Improvements are being made, but the recognition of travel and tourism career patterns has taken a long time to evolve. Much progress is yet to be made in fostering policies to improve tourism education and training, but the prognosis is good. One breakthrough in 1988 was the establishment of the International Academy for the Study of Tourism. This prestigious academy, with a limited membership of some of the worldwide leaders in tourism education, is addressing many of the critical issues in tourism policy. Another major effort toward greater support of tourism policy was launched in 1988–1989 by The George Washington University. This program, called the Tourism Policy Forum, is supported by several international organizations and private sector groups and focuses on international tourism policy issues.

QUALITY TOURISM

In tomorrow's tourism market, consumers will be more sophisticated, demand a higher quality of tourism product, and expect a broader array of specialized travel services. Quality tourism products and services will dominate the international tourism marketplace in the 1990s. Travelers of the future will have even greater ability than they have today to obtain information about more destinations through the use of home computers, videos, and other informational means. Opportunities for learning about specialized travel, whether it be for sports, education, culture, or outer-space exploration, will be at the fingertips of the traveler. More specialized travel services for the international traveler will be available, such as:

- foreign-language-speaking airline personnel, tour guides, maîtres d'hôtel, waiters, telephone operators, hotel concierges, and reception desk, room service, and cashier personnel

- foreign-language tour cassettes, menus, hotel safety, laundry, security, and instruction forms, and aircraft evacuation guides

- universal-symbol direction signs in airports, train and bus terminals, and public facilities such as convention centers, museums, and concert halls

- foreign currency exchange facilities

- special cuisine to accommodate the religious considerations or personal preferences of foreign visitors

The question remains which countries of the world will be ready to provide the services demanded by the increased number of sophisticated visitors from abroad, for those that are not will lose market share to the competition. Future quality will demand increased policy flexibility and continuous short-cycle innovation and improvements. For accommodating the international visitor, this means being cognizant of language, dietary, and cultural differences. On arrival, international visitors often feel vulnerable and sometimes unwelcome. They may not understand nonsmoking sections in restaurants, dress codes, or slang words. They deserve patience and understanding. It is not only good business to accommodate the needs of the international visitor (since international visitors spend six times as much as domestic tourists do), it is also an opportunity to express a country's hospitality and friendliness. Sensitivity in dealing with such guests is good foreign policy, good business policy, and good humanistic policy.

HEALTH, SECURITY, AND SAFETY IN TOURISM

Health, security, and safety issues in tourism, which are important today, will be even more important policy concerns for national and international agendas in the future. As transportation becomes faster and more places are opened to visitors, the possibilities of getting sick, falling victim to an accident, or becoming a crime statistic will also rise. According to the World Health Organization, somewhere between 20 and 50 percent of all international tourists develop health problems resulting from or connected with travel. Policies to combat sickness, crime, and accidents need to be formulated and acted upon.

Some people will not travel internationally simply because they are afraid of getting sick in a strange place. Most are concerned with the hygienic and sanitation standards applied to food and water. Additionally, there are numerous accounts of ear problems from polluted swimming pools and beaches and irritation and infections from unknown insects. A growing number of nonprofit agencies provide various kinds of services to assist the health-conscious traveler. One example is the International Travel Clinic at Johns Hopkins, which specializes in preventing diseases that commonly and uncommonly plague travelers. Members of the clinic staff, all of whom have lived abroad, offer cultural advice on making sensible choices about what to eat and what to do in case of illness in other countries.

Injuries due to negligence by visitors or as a result of unmarked dangerous facilities are also common. For example, even though international visitors make up a small proportion of visitors to U.S.

National Parks, they account for a large percentage of the accidents. This problem has been partially corrected by placing increased numbers of international-symbol signs and other warnings in potentially dangerous areas.

Another fear for many international visitors is that of personal safety. Such concerns are often related to nervousness about the potential for fire, criminal attack, and terrorism (particularly for business travelers). For example, the bombing of Pan Am Flight 103 on December 21, 1988 (and prior incidents in 1985 and 1986), caused passengers and security experts to rethink the rules for safe air travel. The concern for bodily harm due to assault is a real deterrent to travel. In addition, worrying about the possibility of being robbed causes people to avoid certain destinations or leads to a lesser-quality visit because of possessions left behind. These kinds of concerns have been voiced often enough in international tourism circles to cause tourism policymakers to be gravely concerned. One international policy response was to include some of these concerns in the Tourism Bill of Rights and Tourist Code, adopted (September 1985) by the World Tourism Organization (see Appendix J). The Bill and Code include such references as: "[Article IV (c)] . . . ensure the safety of visitors and the security of their belongings through preventive and protective measures" and "[d] afford the best possible conditions of hygiene and access to health services as well as of the prevention of communicable diseases and accidents." The implementation of such policies is important if international tourism is to grow qualitatively as well as quantitatively.

A CHANGING TOURISM WORLD

As a result of the dramatic changes taking place in Eastern Europe and the Soviet Union, the potential for reshaping a part of the tourism world has arisen. While it is too early to make serious prognostications about this area of the world, some generalizations can be made.

It is clear there is a pent-up demand of Westerners wanting to visit Eastern Europe and the Soviet Union. This phenomenon was already happening with respect to the Soviet Union and to a lesser degree Hungary in 1988–1989. But in 1990–1991 there will be an even greater yearning to travel to Eastern Europe and the Soviet Union. Tourism to this area of the world through 1995 will grow and outpace the ability of the infrastructure and receptive services to accommodate the demand.

However, the mystique and curiosity about Eastern Europe and the Soviet Union could be short-lived if the demand for tourism is not properly matched by a supply of infrastructure. The present in-frastructure is substandard, which often results in major in-conveniences for travelers. Concentration on rectifying this situation must be immediate and comprehensive.

In the 1990s, U.S. companies, Western European firms, and prob-ably the Japanese will build hotels and airport facilities, franchise turnkey operations, install computer reservation systems, and develop tour packages for Eastern Europe and the Soviet Union. It represents a special opportunity for U.S. investors to help develop the tourism infrastructure, but it is not without risk. To reduce some of the risks and barriers, there will likely be more interest in joint venture oppor-tunities and in working toward improvements in the investment codes. There will be more ventures like the arrangement made in building the $65 million Warsaw Marriott Hotel—where Marriott is a 25-percent partner, an Austrian construction company that built the hotel owns 25 percent, and LOT, the Polish international airline, owns the other 50 percent. A similar venture is the recently announced deal where Pan American World Airways and ITT Sheraton Corporation will work with Soviet partners in the first Soviet–American effort to build luxury hotels in Moscow.

From 1990–1995 the demand for tourism will be in the direction of Eastern Europe and the Soviet Union. In percentage terms we will also see a dramatic flow from Eastern Europe and the Soviet Union toward the West. The total numbers will be relatively small, but the percent-age increases will be large because the base from which the percentage calculations are made was so low to begin with.

After 1995, assuming major improvements have been made in most of the economies of these Eastern-bloc countries, we can begin to expect more holiday visitors to long-haul destinations such as the United States. Marketing will not be that important initially, because the pent-up demand is already there. Most of these visitors will already have been motivated through movies, magazines, books, and similar kinds of stimulants; as far as the United States is concerned, these tourists' needs will be in the areas of tourism facilitation and receptive services.

EC '92, GATT, AND TOURISM

Now that the twelve-nation European Community is eliminating non-tariff barriers and integrating their economies, and now that the GATT has agreed to negotiations on trade in services, it is time for the world tourism community to focus on freer and fairer trade in tourism.

In every policy forum possible, whether it be participation in a World Tourism Organization meeting or a special international tourism conference, efforts should be made to discuss policy perspectives for improvements in making the tourism product more accessible to a greater number of people.

A dramatic example, in terms of facilitating greater integration of the total trade market, including tourism, is the creation by 1992 of the single market of the twelve-nation European Community, commonly referred to as EC '92. The 1992 program will result in a single market worth $4 trillion made up of 320 million consumers bound by a single set of regulations and directives. As the European Community moves toward its goal of a single internal market by 1992, the tourism link between the United States and the European Community will become even more important. For the European tourism consumer, the elimination of national barriers and stronger European composition will often result in lower prices, greater facilitation of tourism, and hence increased intra-European travel. The challenges to outside countries will include a changing tourism business environment, stronger competition, and a need for new marketing strategies.

As the EC '92 proceeds, there will be impacts affecting international trade relations currently taking place in the GATT negotiations. Since the Uruguay Round of GATT talks included trade in services, the EC '92 movements might cause attention to focus on a prime component of trade in services, that is, tourism. Governments urgently need to establish general principles and operating rules to reduce restrictions on trade in travel services. Barriers to international travel hamper the growth of international tourism. The value of the international travel market would be greater were it not for the large number of nontariff restrictions. The problems of impediments to travel are complex and have existed for many years, but with the current GATT discussions and the dynamic happenings with respect to EC '92, there is no better time than now to formulate tourism policies aimed at eliminating some of the impediments to international travel.

TOURISM AND PEACE

Tourism can contribute to increased knowledge and understanding between peoples of the world. Increased worldwide tourism will mean greater personal contact with foreign nationals and therefore greater understanding of the social, political and economic patterns of the destinations visited. The opportunities that international travel and tourism provide for developing greater national and international understanding and goodwill cannot be measured, but tourism can develop the international contacts leading to a reduction of international tension and in so doing develop an avenue for friendship and respect among nations. In brief, tourism can provide the moral and intellectual basis for international understanding and interdependence. Tourism policy must chart the course so that the international leaders will recognize that tourism is an important tool leading toward a higher quality of life for mankind. As this book stated at the beginning, "the highest purpose of tourism policy is to integrate the economic, political, cultural, intellectual, and environmental benefits of tourism cohesively with people, destinations, and countries in order to improve the global quality of life and provide a foundation for peace and prosperity." The countries of the world, working through an organization like the World Tourism Organization, can search out venues and circumstances to advocate travel and tourism policies that promote goodwill, mutual understanding, and ultimately peace. A good closing example is the The Columbia Charter on World Peace Through Tourism from *The First Global Conference: Tourism—A Vital Force For Peace* (convened in Vancouver, British Columbia, Canada, October 23–27, 1988) (see Appendix L).

APPENDIX A

MINISTERIAL DECLARATION ON THE URUGUAY ROUND

Ministers, meeting on the occasion of the Special Session of CONTRACTING PARTIES at Punta del Este, have decided to launch Multilateral Trade Negotiations (The Uruguay Round). To this end, they have adopted the following Declaration. The Multilateral Trade Negotiations (MTN) will be open to the participation of countries as indicated in Parts I and II of this Declaration. A Trade Negotiations Committee is established to carry out the Negotiations. The Trade Negotiations Committee shall hold its first meeting not later than 31 October 1986. It shall meet as appropriate at Ministerial level. The Multilateral Trade Negotiations will be concluded within four years.

PART I NEGOTIATIONS ON TRADE IN GOODS

The CONTRACTING PARTIES meeting at Ministerial level

DETERMINED	to halt and reverse protectionism and to remove distortions to trade
DETERMINED	also to preserve the basic principles and to further the objectives of the GATT
DETERMINED	also to develop a more open, viable and durable multilateral trading system
CONVINCED	that such action would promote growth and development
MINDFUL	of the negative effects of prolonged financial and monetary instability in the world economy, the indebtedness of a large number of less-developed contracting parties, and considering the linkage between trade, money, finance and development
DECIDE	to enter into Multilateral Trade Negotiations on trade in goods within the framework and under the aegis of the General Agreement on Tariffs and Trade.

A. Objectives

Negotiations shall aim to:

(i) bring about further liberalization and expansion of world trade to the benefit of all countries, especially less-developed contracting parties, including the improvement of access to markets by the reduction and elimination of tariffs, quantitative restrictions and other non-tariff measures and obstacles;

(ii) strengthen the role of GATT, improve the multilateral trading system based on the principles and rules of the GATT and bring about a wider coverage of world trade under agreed, effective and enforceable multi-lateral disciplines;

(iii) increase the responsiveness of the GATT system to the evolving international economic environment, through facilitating necessary structural adjustment, enhancing the relationship of the GATT with the relevant international organizations and taking account of changes in trade patterns and prospects, including the growing importance of trade in high technology products, serious difficulties in commodity markets and the importance of an improved trading environment providing, *inter alia,* for the ability of indebted countries to meet their financial obligations.

(iv) foster concurrent cooperative action at the national and international levels to strengthen the inter-relationship between trade policies and other economic policies affecting growth and development, and to contribute towards continued, effective and determined efforts to improve the functioning of the international monetary system and the flow of financial and real investment resources to developing countries.

B. General Principles Governing Negotiations

(i) Negotiations shall be conducted in a transparent manner, and consistent with the objectives and commitments agreed in this Declaration and with the principles of the General Agreement in order to ensure mutual advantage and increased benefits to all participants.

(ii) The launching, the conduct and the implementation of the outcome of the negotiation shall be treated as parts of a single undertaking. However, agreements reached at an early stage may be implemented on a provisional or a definitive basis by agreement prior to the formal conclusion of the Negotiations. Early agreements shall be taken into account in assessing the overall balance of the negotiations.

(iii) Balanced concessions should be sought within broad trading areas and subjects to be negotiated in order to avoid unwarranted cross-sectoral demands.

(iv) CONTRACTING PARTIES agree that the principle of differential and more favorable treatment embodied in Part IV and other relevant provisions of the General Agreement and in the Decision of the CONTRACTING PARTIES of 28 November 1979 on Differential and More Favourable Treatment, Reciprocity and Fuller Participation of Developing Countries applies to the negotiations. In the implementation of standstill and rollback, particular care should be given to avoiding disruptive effects on the trade of less-developed contracting parties.

(v) The developed countries do not expect reciprocity for commitments made by them in trade negotiations to reduce or remove tariffs and other barriers to the trade of developing countries, i.e. the developed countries do not expect the developing countries, in the course of trade negotiations, to make contributions which are inconsistent with their individual development, financial and trade needs. Developed contracting parties shall therefore not seek, neither shall less-developed contracting parties be required to make, concessions that are inconsistent with the latter's development, financial and trade needs.

(vi) Less-developed contracting parties expect that their capacity to make contributions or negotiated concessions or take other mutually agreed action under the provisions and procedures of the General Agreement would improve with the progressive development of their economies and improvement in their trade situation and they would accordingly expect to participate more fully in the framework of rights and obligations under the General Agreement.

(vii) Special attention shall be given to the particular situation and problems of the least-developed countries and to the need to encourage positive measures to facilitate expansion of their trading opportunities. Expeditious implementation of the relevant provisions of the 1982 Ministerial Declaration concerning the least-developed countries shall also be given appropriate attention.

C. Standstill and Rollback

Commencing immediately and continuing until the formal completion of the Negotiations, each participant agrees to apply the following commitments:

Standstill

(i) not to take any trade restrictive or distorting measure inconsistent with the provisions of the General Agreement or the Instruments negotiated within the framework of GATT or under its auspices;

(ii) not to take any trade restrictive or distorting measure in the legitimate exercise of its GATT rights, that would go beyond that which is necessary to remedy specific situations, as provided for in the General Agreement and the Instruments referred to in (i) above;

(iii) not to take any trade measures in such a manner as to improve its negotiating positions.

Rollback

(i) that all trade restrictive or distorting measures inconsistent with the provisions of the General Agreement or Instruments negotiated within the framework of GATT or under its auspices, shall be phased out or brought into conformity within an agreed timeframe not later than by the date of the formal completion of the negotiations, taking into account multilateral agreements, undertakings and understandings, including strengthened rules and disciplines, reached in pursuance of the Objectives of the Negotiations;

(ii) there shall be progressive implementation of this commitment on an equitable basis in consultations among participants concerned, including all affected participants. This commitment shall take account of the concerns expressed by any participant about measures directly affecting its trade interests;

(iii) there shall be no GATT concessions requested for the elimination of these measures.

Surveillance of standstill and rollback

Each participant agrees that the implementation of these commitments on standstill and rollback shall be subject to multilateral surveillance so as to ensure that these commitments are being met. The Trade Negotiations Committee will decide on the appropriate mechanisms to carry out the surveillance, including periodic reviews and evaluations. Any participant may bring to the attention of the appropriate surveillance mechanism any actions or omissions it believes to be relevant to the fulfillment of these commitments. These notifications should be addressed to the GATT secretariat which may also provide further relevant information.

D. Subjects for Negotiations

Tariffs

Negotiations shall aim, by appropriate methods, to reduce or, as appropriate, eliminate tariffs including the reduction or elimination of high tariffs and tariff escalation. Emphasis shall be given to the expansion of the scope of tariff concessions among all participants.

Non-tariff Measures

Negotiations shall aim to reduce or eliminate non-tariff measures, including quantitative restrictions, without prejudice to any action to be taken in fulfillment of the rollback commitments.

Tropical Products

Negotiations shall aim at the fullest liberalization of trade in tropical products, including in their processed and semi-processed forms and shall cover both tariff and all non-tariff measures affecting trade in these products.

CONTRACTING PARTIES recognize the importance of trade in tropical products to a large number of less-developed contracting parties and agree that negotiations in this area shall receive special attention, including the timing of the negotiations and the implementation of the results as provided for in B(ii).

Natural Resource-Based Products

Negotiations shall aim to achieve the fullest liberalization of trade in natural resource-based products, including in their processed and semi-processed forms. The negotiations shall aim to reduce or eliminate tariff and non-tariff measures, including tariff escalation.

Textiles and Clothing
Negotiations in the area of textiles and clothing shall aim to formulate modalities that would permit the eventual integration of this sector into GATT on the basis of strengthened GATT rules and disciplines, thereby also contributing to the objective of further liberalization of trade.

Agriculture
CONTRACTING PARTIES agree that there is an urgent need to bring more discipline and predictability to world agricultural trade by correcting and preventing restrictions and distortions including those related to structural surpluses so as to reduce the uncertainty, imbalances and instability in world agricultural markets.

Negotiations shall aim to achieve greater liberalization of trade in agriculture and bring all measures affecting import access and export competition under strengthened and more operationally effective GATT rules and disciplines, taking into account the general principles governing the negotiations, by:

(i) improving market access through, *inter alia,* the reduction of import barriers;

(ii) improving the competitive environment by increasing discipline on the use of all direct and indirect subsidies and other measures affecting directly or indirectly agricultural trade, including the phased reduction of their negative effects and dealing with their causes;

(iii) minimizing the adverse effects that sanitary and phytosanitary regulations and barriers can have on trade in agriculture, taking into account the relevant international agreements.

In order to achieve the above objectives, the negotiating group having primary responsibility for all aspects of agriculture will use the recommendations adopted by the CONTRACTING PARTIES at their Fortieth Session, which were developed in accordance with the GATT 1982 Ministerial Programme and take account of the approaches suggested in the work of the Committee on Trade in Agriculture without prejudice to other alternatives that might achieve the objectives of the Negotiations.

GATT Articles
Participants shall review existing GATT articles, provisions and disciplines as requested by interested contracting parties, and, as appropriate, undertake negotiations

Safeguards
(i) A comprehensive agreement on safeguards is of particular importance to the stengthening of the GATT system and to progress in the MTN's.

(ii) The agreement on safeguards:

● shall be based on the basic principles of the General Agreement;

- shall contain, *inter alia,* the following elements: transparency, coverage, objective criteria for action including the concept of serious injury or threat thereof, temporary nature, degressivity and structural adjustment, compensation and retaliation, notifications, consultation, multilateral surveillance and dispute settlement; and

- shall clarify and reinforce the disciplines of the General Agreement and should apply to all contracting parties.

MTN Agreements and Arrangements
Negotiations shall aim to improve, clarify, or expand, as appropriate, agreements and arrangements negotiated in the Tokyo Round of Multilateral Negotiations.

Subsidies and Countervailing Measures
Negotiations on subsidies and countervailing measures shall be based on a review of Articles VI and XVI and the MTN agreement on subsidies and countervailing measures with the objective of improving GATT disciplines relating to all subsidies and countervailing measures that affect international trade. A negotiating group will be established to deal with these issues.

Dispute Settlement
In order to ensure prompt and effective resolution of disputes to the benefit of all contracting parties, negotiations shall aim to improve and strengthen the rules and the procedures of the dispute settlement process, while recognizing the contribution that would be made by more effective and enforceable GATT rules and disciplines. Negotiations shall include the development of adequate arrangements for overseeing and monitoring of the procedures that would facilitate compliance with adopted recommendations.

Trade-Related Aspects of Intellectual Property Rights, including Trade in Counterfeit Goods
In order to reduce the distortions and impediments to international trade, and taking into account the need to promote effective and adequate protection of intellectual property rights, and to ensure that measures and procedures to enforce intellectual property rights do not themselves become barriers to legitimate trade, the negotiations shall aim to clarify GATT provisions and elaborate as appropriate new rules and disciplines.

Negotiations shall aim to develop a multilateral framework of principles, rules and disciplines dealing with international trade in counterfeit goods, taking into account work already undertaken in the GATT.

These negotiations shall be without prejudice to other complementary initiatives that may be taken in the World Intellectual Property Organization and elsewhere to deal with these matters.

Trade-Related Investment Measures
Following an examination of the operation of GATT Articles related to the trade-restrictive and distorting effects of investment measures, negotiations

should elaborate, as appropriate, further provisions that may be necessary to avoid such adverse effects on trade.

E. Functioning of the GATT System

Negotiations shall aim to develop understandings and arrangements:

(i) to enhance the surveillance in the GATT to enable regular monitoring of trade policies and practices of contracting parties and their impact on the functioning of the multilateral trading system;

(ii) to improve the overall effectiveness and decisionmaking of the GATT as an institution, including, *inter alia,* through involvement of ministers;

(iii) to increase the contribution of the GATT to achieving greater coherence in global economic policy making through strengthening its relationship with other international organizations responsible for monetary and financial matters.

F. Participation

a) Negotiations will be open to:

(1) all contracting parties,

(2) countries having acceded provisionally,

(3) countries applying the GATT on a *de facto* basis having announced, not later than 30 April 1987, their intention to accede to the GATT and to participate in the negotiations,

(4) countries that have already informed the CONTRACTING PARTIES, at a regular meeting of the Council of Representatives, of their intention to negotiate the terms of their membership as a contracting party, and

(5) developing countries that have, by 30 April 1987, initiated procedures for accession to the GATT, with the intention of negotiating the terms of their accession during the course of the negotiations.

b) Participation in negotiations relating to the amendment or application of GATT provisions or the negotiation of new provisions will, however, be open only to contracting parties.

G. Organization of the Negotiations

A Group of Negotiations on Goods (GNG) is established to carry out the programme of negotiations contained in this Part of the Declaration. The GNG shall, *inter alia:*

(i) elaborate and put into effect detailed trade negotiating plans prior to 19 December 1986;

(ii) designate the appropriate mechanism for surveillance of commitments to standstill and rollback;

(iii) establish negotiating groups as required. Because of the interrelationship of some issues and taking fully into account the general principles governing the negotiations as stated in B(iii) above it is recognized that aspects of one issue may be discussed in more than one negotiating group. Therefore each negotiating group should as required take into account relevant aspects emerging in other groups;

(iv) also decide upn inclusion of additional subject matters in the negotiations;

(v) co-ordinate the work of the negotiating groups and supervise the progress of the negotiations. As a guideline not more than two negotiating groups should meet at the same time;

(vi) report to the Trade Negotiations Committee.

In order to ensure effective application of differential and more favourable treatment the GNG shall, before the formal completion of the negotiations, conduct an evaluation of the results attained therein in terms of the Objectives and the General Principles Governing Negotiations as set out in the Declaration, taking into account all issues of interest to less-developed contracting parties.

PART II NEGOTIATIONS ON TRADE IN SERVICES

Ministers also decided, as part of the Multilateral Trade Negotiations, to launch negotiations on trade in Services.

Negotiations in this area shall aim to establish a multilateral framework of principles and rules for trade in services, including elaboration of possible disciplines for individual sectors with a view to expansion of such trade under conditions of transparency and progressive liberalization and a means of promoting economic growth of all trading partners and the development of developing countries. Such framework shall respect the policy objectives of national laws and regulations applying to services and shall take into account the work of relevant international organizations.

GATT procedures and practices shall apply to these negotiations. A Group on Negotiations on Services is established to deal with these matters. Participation in the negotiations under this Part of the Declaration will be open to the same countries as under Part I. GATT secretariat support will be provided, with technical support from other organizations as decided by the Group on Negotiations on Services.

The Group on Negotiations on Services shall report to the Trade Negotiations Committee.

Implementation of Results Under Parts I and II

When the results of the Multilateral Trade Negotiations in all areas have been established, Ministers meeting also on the occasion of a Special Session of CONTRACTING PARTIES shall decide regarding the international implementation of the respective results.

APPENDIX B

Begun and held at the City of Washington on Monday, the fifth day of January, one thousand nine hundred and eighty-one

AN ACT

To amend the International Travel Act of 1961 to establish a national tourism policy, and for other purposes.

Be it enacted by the Senate and House of Representatives of the United States of America in Congress assembled,

SHORT TITLE

SECTION 1. This Act may be cited as the "National Tourism Policy Act".

NATIONAL TOURISM POLICY

Sec. 2. (a) The International Travel Act of 1961 (hereinafter in this Act referred to as the "Act") is amended by striking out the first section and inserting in lieu thereof the following: "That this Act may be cited as the 'International Travel Act of 1961'.

"TITLE I—NATIONAL TOURISM POLICY

"Sec. 101. (a) The Congress finds that—

"(1) the tourism and recreation industries are important to the United States, not only because of the numbers of people they serve and the vast human, financial, and physical resources they employ, but because of the great benefits tourism, recreation, and related activities confer on individuals and on society as a whole;

"(2) the Federal Government for many years has encouraged tourism and recreation implicitly in its statutory commitments to the shorter workyear and to the national passenger transportation system, and explicitly in a number of legislative enactments to promote tourism and support development of outdoor recreation, cultural attractions, and historic and natural heritage resources;

"(3) as incomes and leisure time continue to increase, and as our economic and political systems develop more complex global relationships, tourism and recreation will become ever more important aspects of our daily lives; and

"(4) the existing extensive Federal Government involvement in tourism, recreation, and other related activities needs to be better coordinated to effectively respond to the national interest in tourism and recreation and, where appropriate, to meet the needs of State and local governments and the private sector.

"(b) There is established a national tourism policy to—

"(1) optimize the contribution of the tourism and recreation industries to economic prosperity, full employment, and the international balance of payments of the United States;

"(2) make the opportunity for and benefits of tourism and recreation in the United States universally accessible to residents of the United States and foreign countries and insure that present and future generations are afforded adequate tourism and recreation resources;

"(3) contribute to personal growth, health, education, and intercultural appreciation of the geography, history, and ethnicity of the United States;

"(4) encourage the free and welcome entry of individuals traveling to the United States, in order to enhance international understanding and goodwill, consistent with immigration laws, the laws protecting the public health, and laws governing the importation of goods into the United States;

"(5) eliminate unnecessary trade barriers to the United States tourism industry operating throughout the world;

"(6) encourage competition in the tourism industry and maximum consumer choice through the continued viability of the retail travel agent industry and the independent tour operator industry;

"(7) promote the continued development and availability of alternative personal payment mechanisms which facilitate national and international travel;

"(8) promote quality, integrity, and reliability in all tourism and tourism-related services offered to visitors to the United States;

"(9) preserve the historical and cultural foundations of the Nation as a living part of community life and development, and insure future generations an opportunity to appreciate and enjoy the rich heritage of the Nation;

"(10) insure the compatibility of tourism and recreation with other national interests in energy development and conservation, environmental protection, and the judicious use of natural resources;

"(11) assist in the collection, analysis, and dissemination of data which accurately measure the economic and social impact of tourism to and within the United States, in order to facilitate planning in the public and private sectors; and

"(12) harmonize, to the maximum extent possible, all Federal activities in support of tourism and recreation with the needs of the general public and the States, territories, local governments, and the tourism and recreation industry, and to give leadership to all concerned with tourism, recreation, and national heritage preservation in the United States."

Duties

Sec. 3. (a) The following heading is inserted before section 2 of the Act:

"TITLE II—DUTIES".

(b) Section 2 of the Act (22 U.S.C. 2122) is amended by striking out "purpose of the Act" and inserting in lieu thereof "the national tourism policy established by section 101(b)".

(c) Section 3(a) of the Act (22 U.S.C. 2123(a)) is amended by striking out "section 2" and inserting in lieu thereof "section 201", by striking out "and" at the end of paragraph (6), by striking out the period at the end of paragraph (7) and inserting in lieu thereof a semicolon, and by adding after paragraph (7) the following new paragraphs:

"(8) shall establish facilitation services at major ports-of-entry of the United States;

"(9) shall consult with foreign governments on travel and tourism matters and, in accordance with applicable law, represent United States travel and tourism interests before international and intergovernmental meetings;

"(10) shall develop and administer a comprehensive program relating to travel industry information, data service, training and education, and technical assistance;

"(11) shall develop a program to seek and to receive information on a continuing basis from the tourism industry, including consumer and travel trade associations, regarding needs and interests which should be met by a Federal agency or program and to direct that information to the appropriate agency or program;

"(12) shall encourage to the maximum extent feasible travel to and from the United States on United States carriers;

"(13) shall assure coordination within the Department of Commerce so that, to the extent practicable, all the resources of the Department are used to effectively and efficiently carry out the national tourism policy;

"(14) may only promulgate, issue, rescind, and amend such interpretive rules, general statements of policy, and rules of agency organization, procedure, and practice as may be necessary to carry out this Act; and

"(15) shall develop and submit annually to the Congress, within six weeks of transmittal to the Congress of the President's recommended budget for implementing this Act, a detailed marketing plan to stimulate and encourage travel to the United States during the fiscal year for which such budget is submitted and include in the plan the estimated funding and personnel levels required to implement the plan and alternate means of funding activities under this Act.".

(d)(1) Paragraph (5) of section 3(a) of the Act is amended (A) by striking out "foreign countries." and inserting in lieu thereof "foreign countries;", (B) by striking out "this clause;" and inserting in lieu thereof "this paragraph.", (C) by inserting the last two sentences before the first sentence of subsection (c), and (D) by striking out "this clause" in such sentences and inserting in lieu thereof "paragraph (5) of subsection (a)".

(2) Paragraph (7) of section 3(a) of the Act is amended by striking out "countries. The Secretary is authorized to" and inserting in lieu thereof "countries; and the Secretary may" and by striking out "this clause" and inserting in lieu thereof "this paragraph".

(3) Section 3 of the Act is amended by striking out "clause (5)" each place it appears and inserting in lieu thereof "paragraph (5)".

(c)(1) Sections 2 and 3 of the Act are redesignated as sections 201 and 202, respectively, and section 5 is inserted after section 202 (as so redesignated) and redesignated as section 203.

(2) Section 203 of the Act (as so redesignated) is amended by striking out "semi-annually" and inserting in lieu thereof "annually".

(f) The following section is inserted after section 203 of the Act (as so redesignated):

"Sec. 204. (a) The Secretary is authorized to provide, in accordance with subsections (b) and (c), financial assistance to a region of not less than two States or portions of two States to assist in the implementation of a regional tourism promotional and marketing program. Such assistance shall include—

"(1) technical assistance for advancing the promotion of travel to such region by foreign visitors;

"(2) expert consultants; and

"(3) marketing and promotional assistance.

"(b) Any program carried out with assistance under subsection (a) shall serve as a demonstration project for future program development for regional tourism promotion.

"(c) The Secretary may provide assistance under subsection (a) for a region if the applicant for the assistance demonstrates to the satisfaction of the Secretary that—

"(1) such region has in the past been an area that has attracted foreign visitors, but such visits have significantly decreased;

"(2) facilities are being developed or improved to reattract such foreign visitors;

"(3) a joint venture in such region will increase the travel to such region by foreign visitors;

"(4) such regional programs will contribute to the economic well-being of the region;

"(5) such region is developing or has developed a regional transportation system that will enhance travel to the facilities and attractions within such region; and

"(6) a correlation exists between increased tourism to such region and the lowering of the unemployment rate in such region."

Administration

Sec. 4. (a)(1) The first sentence of section 4 of the Act (22 U.S.C. 2124) is amended to read as follows: "There is established in the Department of Commerce a United States Travel and Tourism Administration which shall be headed by an Under Secretary of Commerce for Travel and Tourism who shall be appointed by the President, by and with the advice and consent of the Senate, and who shall report directly to the Secretary.".

(2) The second sentence of section 4 of the Act is amended by striking out "Assistant Secretary of Commerce for Tourism" and inserting in lieu thereof "Under Secretary of Commerce for Travel and Tourism".

(3) Section 4 of the Act is amended by striking out the last sentence and inserting in lieu thereof the following: "The Secretary shall designate an Assistant Secretary of Commerce for Tourism Marketing who shall be under the supervision of the Under Secretary of Commerce for Travel and Tourism. The Secretary shall delegate to the Assistant Secretary responsibility for the development and submission of the marketing plan required by section 202(a)(15).".

(4) Section 5314 of title 5, United States Code, is amended by striking out "Under Secretary of Commerce" and inserting in lieu thereof "Under Secretary of Commerce and Under Secretary of Commerce for Travel and Tourism".

(b) Section 4 of the Act is amended by inserting "(a)" after "Sec. 4.", and by adding at the end the following:

"(b)(1) The Secretary may not reduce the total number of employees of the United States Travel and Tourism Administration assigned to the offices of the Administration in foreign countries to a number which is less than the total number of employees of the United States Travel Service assigned to offices of the Service in foreign countries in fiscal year 1979.

"(2) In any fiscal year the amount of funds which shall be made available from appropriations under this Act for obligation for the activities of the offices of the United States Travel and Tourism Administration in foreign countries shall not be less than the amount obligated in fiscal year 1980 for the activities of the offices of the United States Travel Service in foreign countries.".

(c)(1) The following heading is inserted before section 4 of the Act:

"TITLE III—ADMINISTRATION".

(2) Section 4 of the Act is redesignated as section 301 and the following new sections are inserted after that section:

"Sec. 302. (a) In order to assure that the national interest in tourism is fully considered in Federal decisionmaking, there is established an interagency coordinating council to be known as the Tourism Policy Council (hereinafter in this section referred to as the 'Council').

"(b)(1) The Council shall consist of—

"(A) the Secretary of Commerce who shall serve as Chairman of the Council;

"(B) the Under Secretary for Travel and Tourism who shall serve as the Vice Chairman of the Council and who shall act as Chairman of the Council in the absence of the Chairman;

"(C) the Director of the Office of Management and Budget or the individual designated by the Director from the Office;

"(D) an individual designated by the Secretary of Commerce from the International Trade Administration of the Department of Commerce;

"(E) the Secretary of Energy or the individual designated by such Secretary from the Department of Energy;

"(F) the Secretary of State or the individual designated by such Secretary from the Department of State;

"(G) the Secretary of the Interior or the individual designated by such Secretary of the National Park Service or the Heritage Conservation and Recreation Service of the Department of the Interior;

"(H) the Secretary of Labor or the individual designated by such Secretary from the Department of Labor; and

"(I) the Secretary of Transportation or the individual designated by such Secretary from the Department of Transportation.

"(2) Members of the Council shall serve without additional compensation, but shall be reimbursed for actual and necessary expenses, including travel expenses, incurred by them in carrying out the duties of the Council.

"(3) Each member of the Council, other than the Vice Chairman, may designate an alternate, who shall serve as a member of the Council whenever the regular member is unable to attend a meeting of the Council or any committee of the Council. The designation by a member of the Council of an alternate under the preceding sentence shall be made for the duration of the member's term on the Council. Any such designated alternate shall be selected from individuals who exercise significant decisionmaking authority in the Federal agency involved and shall be authorized to make decisions on behalf of the member for whom he or she is serving.

"(c)(1) Whenever the Council, or a committee of the Council, considers matters that affect the interests of Federal agencies that are not represented on the Council or the committee, the Chairman may invite the heads of such agencies, or their alternates, to participate in the deliberations of the Council or committee.

"(2) The Council shall conduct its first meeting not later than ninety days after the date of enactment of this section. Thereafter the Council shall meet not less than four times each year.

"(d)(1) The Council shall coordinate policies, programs, and issues relating to tourism, recreation, or national heritage resources involving Federal departments, agencies, or other entities. Among other things, the Council shall—

"(A) coordinate the policies and programs of member agencies that have a significant effect on tourism, recreation, and national heritage preservation;

"(B) develop areas of cooperative program activity;

"(C) assist in resolving interagency program and policy conflicts; and

"(D) seek and receive concerns and views of State and local governments and the Travel and Tourism Advisory Board with respect to Federal programs and policies deemed to conflict with the orderly growth and development of tourism.

"(2) To enable the Council to carry out its functions—

"(A) the Council may request directly from any Federal department or agency such personnel, information, services, or facilities, on a compensated or uncompensated basis, as he determines necessary to carry out the functions of the Council;

"(B) each Federal department or agency shall furnish the Council with such information, services, and facilities as it may request to the extent permitted by law and within the limits of available funds; and

"(C) Federal agencies and departments may, in their discretion, detail to temporary duty with the Council, such personnel as the Council may request for carrying out the functions of the Council, each such detail to be without loss of seniority, pay, or other employee status.

"(3) The Administrator of the General Services Administration shall provide administrative support services for the Council on a reimbursable basis.

"(e) The Council shall establish such policy committees as it considers necessary and appropriate, each of which shall be comprised of any or all of the members of the Council and representatives from Federal departments, agencies, and instrumentalities not represented on the Council. Each such policy committee shall be designed—

"(1) to monitor a specific area of Federal Government activity, such as transportation, energy and natural resources, economic development, or other such activities related to tourism; and

"(2) to review and evaluate the relation of the policies and activities of the Federal Government in that specific area to tourism, recreation, and national heritage conservation in the United States.

"(f) The Council shall submit an annual report for the preceding fiscal year to the President for transmittal to Congress on or before the thirty-first day of December of each year. The report shall include—

"(1) a comprehensive and detailed report of the activities and accomplishments of the Council and its policy committees;

"(2) the results of Council efforts to coordinate the policies and programs of member agencies that have a significant effect on tourism, recreation, and national heritage preservation, resolve interagency conflicts, and develop areas of cooperative program activity;

"(3) an analysis of problems referred to the Council by State and local governments, the tourism industry, the Secretary of Commerce, or any of the Council's policy committees along with a detailed statement of any actions taken or anticipated to be taken to resolve such problems; and

"(4) such recommendations as the Council deems appropriate.

"Sec. 303. (a) There is established the Travel and Tourism Advisory Board (hereinafter in this section referred to as the 'Board') to be composed of fifteen members appointed by the Secretary. The members of the Board shall be appointed as follows:

"(1) Not more than eight members of the Board shall be appointed from the same political party.

"(2) The members of the Board shall be appointed from among citizens of the United States who are not regular full-time employees of the United States and shall be selected for appointment so as to provide as nearly as practicable a broad representation of different geographical regions within the United States and of the diverse and varied segments of the tourism industry.

"(3) Twelve of the members shall be appointed from senior executive officers of organizations engaged in the travel and tourism industry. Of such members—

"(A) at least one shall be a senior representative from a labor organization representing employees of the tourism industry; and

"(B) at least one shall be a representative of the States who is knowledgeable of tourism promotion.

"(4) Of the remaining three members of the Board—

(A) one member shall be a consumer advocate or ombudsman from the organized public interest community;

"(B) one member shall be an economist, statistician, or accountant; and

"(C) one member shall be an individual from the academic community who is knowledgeable in tourism, recreation, or national heritage conservation.

The Secretary shall serve as an ex officio member of the Board. The duration of the Board shall not be subject to the Federal Advisory Committee Act. A list of the members appointed to the Board shall be forwarded by the Secretary to the Senate Committee on Commerce, Science, and Transportation and the House Committee on Energy and Commerce.

"(b) The members of the Board shall be appointed for a term of office of three years, except that of the members first appointed—

"(1) four members shall be appointed for terms of one year, and (2) four members shall be appointed for terms of two years, as designated by the Secretary at the time of appointment. Any member appointed to fill a vacancy occurring before the expiration of the term for which the member's predecessor was appointed shall be appointed only for the remainder of such term. A member may serve after the expiration of his term until his successor has taken office. Vacancies on the Board shall be filled in the same manner in which the original appointments were made. No member of the Board shall be eligible to serve in excess of two consecutive terms of three years each.

"(c) The Chairman and Vice Chairman and other appropriate officers of the Board shall be elected by and from members of the Board other than the Secretary.

"(d) The members of the Board shall receive no compensation for their services as such, but shall be allowed such necessary travel expenses and per diem as are authorized by section 5703 of title 5, United States Code. The Secretary shall pay the reasonable and necessary expenses incurred by the Board in connection with the coordination of Board activities, announcement and reporting of meetings, and preparation of such reports as are required by subsection (f).

"(e) The Board shall meet at least semi-annually and shall hold such other meetings at the call of the Chairman, the Vice Chairman, or a majority of its members.

"(f) The Board shall advise the Secretary with respect to the implementation of this Act and shall advise the Assistant Secretary for Tourism Marketing with respect to the preparation of the marketing plan under section 202(a)(15). The Board shall prepare an annual report concerning its activities and include therein such recommendations as it deems appropriate with respect to the performance of the Secretary under this Act and the operation and effectiveness of programs under this Act. Each annual report shall cover a fiscal year and shall be submitted on or before the thirty-first day of December following the close of the fiscal year.".

Authorizations

Sec. 5 (a) Section 6 of the Act (22 U.S.C. 2126) is redesignated as section 304 and the first sentence is amended to read as follows: "For the purpose of carrying out this Act there is authorized to be appropriated an amount not to exceed $8,600,000 for the fiscal year ending September 30, 1982.".

(b) Section 7 of the Act (22 U.S.C. 2127) is redesignated as section 305 and sections 8 and 9 of the Act (22 U.S.C. 2128) are repealed.

Effective Date

Sec. 6. The amendments made by this Act shall take effect October 1, 1981.

APPENDIX C

AGREEMENT BETWEEN THE UNITED STATES OF AMERICA AND THE UNITED MEXICAN STATES ON THE DEVELOPMENT AND FACILITATION OF TOURISM

CONSIDERING that the United States of America and the United Mexican States share an extended border and have developed close neighborly and commercial relations;

RECOGNIZING that international cooperation and economic exchange should serve to foster man's development, to enhance mutual respect for human dignity, and to promote common welfare;

ACKNOWLEDGING that the promotion of tourism is considered a legitimate diplomatic and consular function;

CONVINCED that tourism, because of its socio-cultural and economic dynamics, is an excellent instrument for promoting economic development, understanding, goodwill, and close relations between peoples;

NOTING that a valuable structure for tourism, already existing between both countries, stands ready for further development;

The Governments of the United States of America and of the United Mexican States (the Parties) agree to conclude a Tourism Agreement which, within their respective legal frameworks, will promote the objectives stated in the following provisions;

ARTICLE I

Government Tourism Offices and Personnel

1. In conformance with the laws, regulations, polities and procedures of the host Party, each Party;

   a. May establish and operate official travel promotion offices in the territory of the other Party, and,

   b. Agrees to accredit as members of a diplomatic or consular post tourism officials of the other Party.

2. Such tourism personnel shall perform traditional diplomatic or consular functions (e.g., the officials do not perform commercial transactions, including making airline or other travel arrangements or performing other similar services normally provided by travel agencies).

ARTICLE II

Development of the Tourism Industry and Infrastructure

1. The Parties, subject to their laws, will facilitate and encourage the activities of tourism service providers such as travel agents, tour wholesalers and operators, hotel chains, airlines, railroads, motor coach operators, and steamship companies generating two-way tourism between their countries.

2. Each Party will,

    a. Permit air, sea and surface carriers of the other Party, whether public or private, to open sales agencies and to appoint representatives in its territory in order to market their services;

    b. In accordance with the bilateral Air Transport Agreement, encourage the carriers of the other Party to develop and promote, through designated and authorized sales outlets in its territory, departures from their own territories with special or excursion fares designed to encourage reciprocal tourist travel;

    c. Permit the sale of promotional transportation tickets for use in the territory of one Party by carriers of the other Party through authorized outlets in its territory;

    d. Expedite, to the extent possible, the award to carriers of new air routes established under the bilateral Air Transport Agreement signed by both countries; and

    e. In accordance with overall discussions and negotiations between the two countries, initiate substantive dialogue on motor carrier issues which impact on tourism.

3. To the extent that either Party is subject to statutes imposing duty on the entrance of ticket stock or sales materials of the carriers or tourism enterprises of the other, that Party shall review those statutes with the objective of providing for the eventual duty-free entry of such materials on a reciprocal basis.

ARTICLE III

Facilitation and Documentation

1. The Parties will endeavor to facilitate travel of tourists into both countries by simplifying and eliminating, as appropriate, procedural and documentary requirements.

2. Each Party shall facilitate, to the extent permitted by its laws, the entry of performers and artists who:

    a. Are nationals of the other Party; and

b. Have been invited to participate in international cultural events to be held in its territory.

3. Each Party shall take all necessary facilitative measures to encourage binational cultural events which would strengthen ties and promote tourism.

4. The Parties will consult on the opening of additional border crossing points and on the designation of such points as high priority based on the needs of touristic development of each area.

5. The Parties will encourage the training of personnel at ports of entry and elsewhere within their respective territories so that tourists' rights are respected and tourists of both countries are extended all appropriate courtesies.

6. The Parties shall consider, on the basis of reciprocity, and on official request, waiving applicable visa fees for the entry and exit of teachers and experts in the field of tourism.

7. Aware of the importance of automobile collision and liability coverage to automobile tourism between the two countries, the Parties shall publicize in the territory of the other, in accordance with applicable regulations in each country, the respective automobile insurance requirements, either by distributing information through their respective national tourist offices or by other appropriate means.

8. Both Parties recognize the necessity of promoting, within their respective facilities and administrative capabilities, the health and safety of tourists from the other country, whether traveling by automobile or any other means of transportation, and will either provide information about available medical services or encourage government and non-government organizations or agencies to do so as needed.

9. Both Parties recognize the need for promoting and facilitating, where possible, investment by American and Mexican investors in their tourism sectors.

10. The Parties shall consult with each other, as appropriate, in their multilateral efforts to reduce or eliminate barriers to international tourism.

ARTICLE IV
Cultural and Tourism Programs

1. The Parties regard it appropriate to encourage tourist and cultural activities designed to strengthen the ties between the peoples and to improve the overall quality of life of the inhabitants of both countries and will consider exchange programs which are consistent with the cultural heritage of each country.

2. The Parties will consider it a priority to promote travel to developing

regions which contain examples of the native culture of each country, and to develop and improve tourist facilities and attractions in those areas.

3. The Parties will encourage the balanced and objective presentation of their respective historic and socio-cultural heritage and promote respect for human dignity and conservation of cultural, archaeological, and ecological resources.

4. The Parties will exchange information concerning the use of facilities for shows and exhibitions in their countries.

ARTICLE V

Tourism Training

1. The Parties consider it desirable to encourage their respective experts to exchange technical information and/or documents in the following fields;

   a. Systems and methods to prepare teachers and instructors in technical matters, particularly with respect to procedures for facilitation, hotel operation and administration:

   b. Scholarships for teachers, instructors, and students;

   c. Curricula and study programs to train personnel who provide tourism services; and

   d. Curricula and study programs for hotel schools.

2. Each Party will encourage their respective students and professors of tourism to take advantage of fellowships offered by colleges, universities, and training centers of the other.

ARTICLE VI

Tourism Statistics

1. Both Parties will do what is possible to improve the reliability and compatibility of statistics on tourism between the two countries, in both the border and interior regions.

2. The Parties agree to establish a technical committee on tourism statistics in which the appropriate agencies of both countries shall participate.

   a. The committee shall address itself to the exchange and reconciliation of statistical data measuring tourism between the two countries and to the improvement of collecting such data.

   b. The committee will consider the conduct of joint research studies.

   c. The committee shall meet alternately in the United States and Mexico at least twice a year.

3. The Parties consider it desirable to exchange information on the size and

characteristics of the actual and potential tourism markets in their two countries.

4. The Parties agree that the guidelines on the collection and presentation of domestic and international tourism statistics established by the World Tourism Organization shall constitute the requirements for such a data base.

ARTICLE VII
Joint Marketing of Tourism

1. Subject to budgetary limitations, the Parties shall consider the conduct of joint marketing activities in third countries.

2. Activities which shall receive consideration include joint operation of inspection trips for tour wholesalers and operators, and journalists from third countries, film festivals, travel trade shows and travel missions.

ARTICLE VIII
World Tourism Organization

1. The Parties shall work within the World Tourism Organization to develop, and encourage the adoption of, uniform standards and recommended practices which, if applied by governments, would facilitate tourism.

2. The Parties shall assist one another in matters of cooperation and effective participation in the World Tourism Organization.

ARTICLE IX
Consultations

1. The Parties agree that tourism and tourism matters shall be discussed, as appropriate, in bilateral consultations attended by representatives of their official tourism organizations. These meetings shall be held alternately in the United States and Mexico at least once a year.

2. Whenever possible these consultations will be held in conjunction with other meetings of the United States of America and the United Mexican States. Both Parties will consider the possibility of establishing working groups to consider specific issues or articles of the Agreement.

3. The consultations to be undertaken under this Agreement constitute a part of the efforts to improve bilateral cooperation in the framework of the U.S.–Mexico Binational Commission. Therefore, both Parties shall report periodically to the Binational Commission on their programs, results and recommendations.

4. The United Mexican States designates the Tourism Secretariat as its agency with primary responsibility for implementing this Agreement for Mexico.

5. The United States of America designates the U.S. Department of Commerce as its agency with primary responsibility for implementing this Agreement for the United States.

ARTICLE X
Protocols

1. The Parties may implement this Agreement through protocols. Protocols may cover subjects such as cooperative activities to facilitate tourism, tourism training, joint marketing, development of tourism statistics, funding, procedures to be followed in such joint projects, and other appropriate matters.

2. The cost of all activities under this article shall be mutually agreed upon. These expenses for such activities will be borne subject to all applicable laws and regulations and to the availability of human and financial resources.

ARTICLE XI
Tourism Agreement of 1983 Superseded

This Agreement shall supersede and replace the Tourism Agreement between the Parties, signed April 18, 1983.

ARTICLE XII
Period of Effectiveness

1. Each Party shall inform the other by way of diplomatic note of the completion of necessary legal requirements in its country for entry into force of the present Agreement. The Agreement shall enter into force upon receipt of such notification by the second Party.

2. Upon entry into force, this Agreement shall be valid for a period of five years and will be renewed automatically for additional periods of five years unless either Party expresses objection in writing, through diplomatic channels three months prior to the expiration date.

3. The Agreement shall be terminated ninety days after either Party transmits written notice of its intention to terminate to the other Party.

ARTICLE XIII
Notification

After entry into force, both Parties agree to notify the Secretariat General of the World Tourism Organization of this Agreement and any subsequent amendments.

DONE at Washington, D.C. this third day of October, 1989 in two originals in the English and Spanish languages, both texts being equally authentic.

APPENDIX D

AGREEMENT BETWEEN THE GOVERNMENT OF THE UNITED STATES OF AMERICA AND THE GOVERNMENT OF THE REPUBLIC OF VENEZUELA ON THE DEVELOPMENT AND FACILITATION OF TOURISM

The Government of the United States of America and the Government of the Republic of Venezuela considering:

1. That close ties have existed between the United States of America and the Republic of Venezuela for many years and that these ties should be preserved and strengthened;

2. That international cooperation should serve to foster man's development, to enhance mutual respect for human dignity, and to promote shared well-being;

3. That tourism, because of its socio-cultural and economic dynamics, is an excellent instrument for promoting economic development, understanding, goodwill, and close relations between people;

4. The importance of private sector investment and trained personnel in the field of tourism;

5. That both countries retain a national interest in the facilitation of tourism development; and

6. That both countries are members of the World Tourism Organization;

Have agreed to conclude this Agreement which, within the respective Parties' legal frameworks, will promote the objectives stated in the following provisions.

ARTICLE I
Travel Promotion Offices

1. Each Party may establish and operate, subject to applicable laws and regulations and by mutual consent of the Parties, travel promotion offices in the territory of the other Party.

2. Each Party agrees, on a numerically reciprocal basis, to accredit as members of the Diplomatic Mission or Consular Post, the persons that the other party designates to perform the activities in the Tourism Promotion Offices, in conformance with the laws, regulations and policies of the host country.

3. Travel promotion offices opened by either Party shall be operated on a non-profit basis and officials will not perform commercial transactions, or

149

any other service normally provided by Travel Agents. Such offices shall not sell services to the public or otherwise compete with private sector travel agents or tour operators of the host country. Personnel assigned to such offices may engage in promotion, liaison, negotiation, and advisory activities including:

a) Providing information about the tourist facilities and attractions in their respective countries to the public, the travel trade, and the media;

b) Conducting meetings and workshops for representatives of the travel industry;

c) Distributing posters, window displays, and other sales aids;

d) Coordinating advertising campaigns and engaging in cooperative advertising and other promotional activites;

e) Organizing familiarization tours of their respective tourist facilities for tour operators. travel agents, and media representatives of the host country;

f) Participating in trade shows; and

g) Performing market research.

However, nothing in this provision shall obligate either Party to open such offices in the territory of the other.

ARTICLE II
Facilitation of Tourism

1. The Parties will endeavor to facilitate travel of tourists into both countries.

2. The parties shall work with relevant international organizations to develop, and encourage the adoption of, uniform standards and recommended practices which, if applied by Governments, would facilitate international tourism.

3. The Parties shall facilitate the holding of congresses and conventions in each other's territory and the attendance of their citizens in such congresses and conventions, especially those pertaining to educational, scientific, technological, professional, business, tourism, social, and cultural matters.

ARTICLE III
Exchanges and Mutual Assistance

1. The parties shall encourage cooperation between tourism authorites and organizations, and regions and cities of the two countries in order to increase mutual tourist traffic and cooperation in the field of tourism in general.

2. Cooperation may include

    a) efforts to identify tourism experts for short term exchange assignments; and

    b) the identification of volunteer private sector executives, and instructors and professors of tourism who are eligible for sabbatical leave, who might be available to

        (1) instruct personnel designated by the other Party in a structured training program; and

        (2) evaluate the training methods employed by the other Party.

3. The Governments of the United States of America and of the Republic of Venezuela accept the importance of conservation and management of natural and historical sites of national and international significance, and shall continue to take necessary steps toward this end.

4. Recognizing, in the context of this Agreement, the important economic benefits of tourism that can be associated with sites referred to in paragraph 3 above, National Park Institute, Ministry of the Environment and Renewable Natural Resources of the Republic of Venezuela and the National Park Service, U.S. Department of the Interior, may enter into exploratory discussions regarding opportunities for information exchanges, training, and technical cooperation in the planning, preservation and management of national parks and protected natural, historical, archaeological, and recreational sites and in related, cooperative activities. If these discussions lead to concrete proposals, it is considered the possibility of signing a separate agreement between the National Park Service and the Instituto Nacional de Parques.

5. The Parties, through their competent authorities and other organizations, shall endeavor to develop new opportunities for commerce in tourism-related projects and for joint ventures in the establishment of tourism facilities and infrastructure.

ARTICLE IV

Education and Training

The Parties consider it desirable to encourage their respective experts to exchange appropriate information in the following fields:

a) Systems and methods to prepare teachers and instructors, particularly with regard to procedures for facilitating hotel operation and administration, marketing, congress management, and other tourism services;

b) Tourism scholarships for teachers, instructors, and students; and

c) Curricular and study programs for tourism and hotel schools.

ARTICLE V

Tourism Statistics and Research

1. The Parties agree that the competent authorities of the two countries should endeavor to improve the reliability and comparability of their tourism statistics by using the Guidelines on the Collection and Presentation of International Tourism Statistics applied by the World Tourism Organization.

2. The Parties consider it desirable for their competent authorities to exchange information about the tourism markets in the two countries.

ARTICLE VI

Tourism Safety and Security

Both Parties recognize the necessity of promoting, within their respective capabilities, the health and safety of foreign tourists.

ARTICLE VII

Exchange of Information

The Parties will facilitate the exchange of information between authorities, agencies, and organizations and will support each other's efforts to promote and facilitate the following:

   a) Investment opportunities by American and Venezuelan investors in their tourism sectors;

   b) The promotion and marketing of tourism; and

   c) Conservation of archaeological, ecological, and cultural resources.

ARTICLE VIII

Consultation and Implementation

1. The Parties shall consult and assist one another in matters of cooperation and effective participation in the World Tourism Organization.

2. The United States of America designates the U.S. Travel and Tourism Administration as its competent authority with primary responsibility for implementing this Agreement for the United States.

3. The Republic of Venezuela designates the Corpoturismo as its agency with primary responsibility for implementing this Agreement for the Republic of Venezuela.

4. All activities under this Agreement are subject to the applicable laws and regulations of the Parties and are subject to the availability of appropriated funds and personnel.

ARTICLE IX
Period of Effectiveness and Amendments

1. This Agreement shall enter into force on the date of signature.

2. The Agreement shall be valid for a period of five years and will be automatically renewed for additional periods of five years unless either Party expesses objection in writing, through diplomatic channels, ninety days prior to expiry.

3. This Agreement may be terminated by either Party ninety days after that Party transmits written notice of intention to terminate to the other Party.

4. Neither the expiration nor termination of this Agreement shall affect the validity or duration of projects already in progress hereunder.

5. The Agreement may be amended by written consent of both Parties.

ARTICLE X
Notification

After entry into force, both Parties agree to notify the Secretariat General of the World Tourism Organization of this Agreement and any subsequent amendments.

DONE at New York City this twenty-seventh day of September 1989 in two originals in the English and Spanish languages, both texts being equally authentic.

APPENDIX E

JOINT COMMUNIQUÉ OF ROBERT A. MOSBACHER, SECRETARY OF COMMERCE OF THE UNITED STATES OF AMERICA AND CARLOS HANK GONZALEZ, SECRETARY OF TOURISM OF THE UNITED MEXICAN STATES, NOVEMBER 21, 1989

The Secretary of Commerce of the United States of America, Robert A. Mosbacher, and the Secretary of Tourism of the United Mexican States, Carlos Hank Gonzalez, met today to begin discussions on the implementation process of the *Agreement* between the United States of America and the United Mexican States on the *Development and Facilitation of Tourism*.

This Agreement was signed in Washington, D.C. on October 3, 1989, the signing being witnessed by President George Bush and President Carlos Salinas de Gortari during the latter's official visit to the United States. The Agreement cites the strong neighborly and commercial relations between the two countries and recognizes the importance of tourism as an excellent instrument for promoting economic development, understanding, goodwill, and close relations between peoples.

During their meeting the discussions largely focused on Article III of the Agreement. Among other items, this article highlights that both countries ". . . recognize the need for promoting and facilitating, where possible, investment by American and Mexican investors in their tourism sectors." Both Secretaries brought together key business leaders and government officials for the purpose of a positive exchange of information and discussion on investment opportunities in tourism projects which will benefit both countries.

During this meeting the two Secretaries also recognized that Article VI of the Agreement on "Tourism Statistics" was being implemented. The Agreement provides for establishing a technical committee to work toward the improvement of ". . . the reliability and compatibility of statistics on tourism between the two countries. . . ." The technical committee convoked its meeting today under the auspices of the Agreement.

The two Secretaries noted that tourism is a positive instrument which can and should be used to improve the quality of life for all peoples and that it is a vital force for achieving peace and international understanding. They noted that this work should provide significant opportunities to enhance mutual understanding and lead to joint projects which will benefit both countries.

Secretary Mosbacher and Secretary Hank Gonzalez agreed that the above measures will contribute toward the continued development of a sound and vibrant tourism relationship between the United States and Mexico. Both Secretaries expressed their governments' determination to build on the framework of the current relationship between the two countries and to add to the accomplishments already made.

APPENDIX F

UNITED STATES–CANADA FREE-TRADE AGREEMENT
SECTORAL ANNEXES

B. TOURISM SERVICES
Article 1: Scope and Coverage

1. This Sectoral Annex shall apply to any measure related to trade in tourism services.

2. For purposes of this Sectoral Annex:

   tourism services include the tourism-related activities of the following: travel agency and related travel services including tour wholesaling, travel counselling, arranging and booking; issuance of travellers' insurance; all modes of international passenger transportation; hotel reservation services; terminal services for all modes of transport, including concessions; transportation catering services; airport transfer; lodging, including hotels, motels, and rooming houses; local sightseeing, regardless of mode of transportation; intercity tour operation; guide and interpreter services; automobile rental; provision of resort facilities; rental of recreational equipment; food services; retail services; organizational and support services for international conventions; marina-related services including the fueling, supply, and repair of, and provision of docking space to, pleasure boats; recreational vehicle rental; campground and trailer park services; amusement park services; commercial tourist attractions; and tourism-related services of a financial nature;

   tourism-related services of a financial nature means such services provided by an entity that is not a financial institution as defined in Article 1706; and

   trade in tourism services means the provision of a tourism service by a person of a Party

   a) within the territory of that Party to a visitor who is a resident of the other Party, or

   b) within the territory of the other Party to a resident of, or visitor to, the other Party, either cross-border, through a commercial presence or through an establishment in the territory of the other Party.

Article 2: Obligations

1. This Chapter shall apply to all measures related to trade in tourism services, which measures include:

a) provision of tourism services in the territory of a Party, either individually or with members of a travel industry trade association;

b) appointment, maintenance and commission of agents or representatives in the territory of a Party to provide tourism services;

c) establishment of sales offices or designated franchises in the territory of a Party; and

d) access to basic telecommunications transport networks.

2. Provided that such promotional activities do not include the provision of tourism services for profit, each Party may promote officially in the territory of the other Party the travel and tourism opportunities in its own territory, including engagement in joint promotions with tourism enterprises of that Party and provincial, state and local governments.

3. The Parties recognize that the adoption or application of fees or other charges on the departure or arrival of tourists from their territories impedes the free flow of tourism services. When such fees or other charges are imposed, they shall be applied in a manner consistent with Article 1402 and limited in amount to the approximate cost of the services rendered.

4. Neither Party shall impose, except in conformity with Article VIII of the *Articles of Agreement of the International Monetary Fund,* restrictions on the value of tourism services that its residents or visitors to its territory may purchase from persons of the other Party.

Article 3: Relationship to the Agreement

Nothing in this Sectoral Annex shall be construed as:

a) conferring rights or imposing obligations on a Party relating to computer services and enhanced services as defined in Annex 1404(C), financial services as defined in Article 1706 and transportation services that are not otherwise conferred or imposed pursuant to any other provision of this Agreement and its annexes; or

b) affecting in any way the application of measures relating to the provision of tourism-related services of a financial nature.

Article 4: Consultation

The Parties shall consult at least once a year to:

a) identify and seek to eliminate impediments to trade in tourism services; and

b) identify ways to facilitate and increase tourism between the Parties.

APPENDIX G

NOVEMBER 27, 1989
MEETING OF THE U.S.–CANADA TRADE COMMISSION
NOVEMBER 30, 1989

REPORT BY THE WORKING GROUP ON TOURISM
Highlights

Since its establishment by the Commission, the Working Group on Tourism held its first meeting in Washington on November 27, 1989. The two countries' bilateral trade in tourism has been an essentially free trade relationship pre-dating the Free Trade Agreement. The FTA ratified the status quo, clearly identified the importance of tourism in the countries' bilateral trade, and provided a framework for facilitating the development of tourism within the free trade area.

There were no trade issues to be discussed at the first meeting of the Working Group. The Group therefore focused on the exchange of information on major policy and initiatives proposals and agreed to undertake joint actions in a number of areas of mutual interest to both countries.

Specifically, the Group noted that the two countries concluded a bilateral Memorandum of Understanding on Tourism Research in June of 1986 that has been mutually beneficial. The delegations agreed to examine opportunities for joint tourism research and explore new areas of research activity that could be covered under their bilateral Memorandum of Understanding on Tourism Research. The Group concluded that it would be desirable to consult on matters of mutual concern coming before international tourism organizations such as the World Tourism Organization, the Tourism Committee of the Organization for Economic Cooperation and Development and the Tourism Committee of the Organization of American States.

The U.S. delegation agreed to participate in the Steering Committee for the World Tourism Organization's 1990 Conference on Tourism Statistics, which will be held in Ottawa and hosted by the Canadian Government. The Conference will be the first international meeting on tourism statistics held under WTO auspices since 1963 and will update and redefine standards and definitions for the collection of international visitor statistics. Given the dramatic growth of tourism worldwide and the more diversified types of firms that comprise the tourism industry of the nineties, the group agreed to work together to ensure the Conference's success.

The two delegations also agreed that revisions to the International Standard Industrial Classification System are urgently needed to more accurately reflect the economic significance of the tourism industry in national accounts. Both delegations agreed to participate within the Steering Committee to ensure that this issue is considered by the Conference.

The Group discussed the European Communities' planned economic integration by 1992 (EC '92). The two delegations agreed to share information on the anticipated impact of the integration of EC tourism enterprises on the North American tourism industry and on the ability of the North American industry to compete successfully for tourism business in the new environment of the future.

The Canadian delegation informed the U.S. delegation about Canada's overall tax reforms and the implications for the tourism industries of both countries. The Canadian delegation agreed to a request to provide information for the U.S. side about the status of any tax that would apply to international air tickets purchased in Canada.

The Canadian delegation advised the U.S. delegation of an impediment to attracting U.S. participation in trade shows and conventions held in Canada: goods owned by U.S. companies but not manufactured in the United States are treated as dutiable by the U.S. Customs Service (on re-entry to the U.S.) even though duty has been collected on them at the time of initial entry. The U.S. delegation agreed to investigate the practice with the U.S. Customs Service and possibly the U.S. Department of Transportation's interagency Facilitation Committee.

The Group acknowledged the work of the National Travel and Tourism Awareness Council in publicizing the economic importance and benefits of tourism and agreed to encourage the two countries' respective private sector associations to undertake joint activites in observation of annual tourism awareness week, held the third week in May.

The Group agreed to hold its second meeting in Canada and to consider convening that meeting during tourism awareness week.

APPENDIX H

DECLARATION OF RIO DE JANEIRO

THE INTER-AMERICAN TRAVEL CONGRESS AT ITS FIRST SPECIAL MEETING HELD IN RIO DE JANEIRO DURING THE SESQUICENTENNIAL OF THE INDEPENDENCE OF BRAZIL AND THE TOURISM YEAR OF THE AMERICAS

CONSIDERING:

That tourism is a cultural, economic, and social force, whose impact on all sectors of society is universally recognized, since it brings into contract peoples of dissimilar background and standards of living, strengthening relationships, dispelling prejudice, and eschewing arrogance; and that the tourist is an ambassador of the culture of his country, who at the same time, assimilates the culture with which he comes into contract;

That tourism, in supporting efforts to achieve hemispheric integration and the pursuit of economic goals, complements the high aims of peace and cooperation among the American nations;

The great economic, social and cultural importance of tourism to the overall and balanced development of the American hemisphere, and that joint action should be taken to ensure a continuing vigorous and rapid development of tourism in the region,

RESOLVES:

To make the following declaration of purposes:

i. To integrate tourism programs effectively into the economic and social development process, thus rationalizing tourism investments and initiatives by creating new tourist areas.

ii. To give priority within the American Hemisphere to strengthening regional tourism, thus facilitating marketing activities throughout the world.

iii. To strengthen domestic tourism so that greater numbers of persons in each country may take advantage of opportunities for rest and recreation, thus converting this type of tourism into an effective instrument of national unification and a powerful medium for achieving cultural development.

iv. To foster the economic integration and development of the American Hemisphere, leading to greater mutual understanding among its peoples and stimulating more investments in tourism in both the public and private sectors.

   v. To encourage international cooperation for the overall organization of tourism in the Americas, identifying areas of the hemisphere in which tourism should be given priority with a view to promoting a redistribution of income and correcting regional differences in development.

  vi. To modernize tourism programs, on a continuing basis, keeping pace with constant changes in the market brought about by new technologies, expansion of mass transportation, and improvement of world-wide communications, so that the tourist may be provided with greater facilities for access and better services.

 vii. To consider as priority measures within the tourism development programs of the American governments and the regional and international organizations the carrying out of specific projects within the fields of human resources, promotion, organization, information, research, and technical assistance.

viii. To stimulate private enterprise and use tourism resources intelligently as a means of realizing the potential of tourism as a stimulant to economic growth.

  ix. To stimulate public and private enterprise to meet the growing demands of the tourist market for improved services and up-to-date operational methods.

   x. To implement multinational programs designed to prevent the problems arising from mass tourism, such as environmental pollution, and contribute to the conservation and enhancement of each country's historic, artistic, and archaelogical heritage and of its beauties, which programs should be integrated within the development plans of the American States.

APPENDIX I

MANILA DECLARATION ON WORLD TOURISM

The World Tourism Conference,

Held at Manila, Philippines, from 27 September to 10 October 1980, convened by the World Tourism Organization with the participation of 107 delegations of States and 91 delegations of observers, in order to clarify the real nature of tourism in all its aspects and the role tourism is bound to play in a dynamic and vastly changing world, as well as to consider the responsibility of States for the development and enhancement of tourism in present-day societies as more than a purely economic activity of nations and peoples,

Noting with satisfaction the addresses of His Excellency Ferdinand E. Marcos, President of the Republic of the Philippines, and Madame Imelda Romualdez Marcos, Governor of Metropolitan Manila and Minister of Human Settlements, as well as the messages of the Heads of State and of Government to the Conference, the statements of delegations and the report of the Secretary-General of the World Tourism Organization,

Considering that world tourism can develop in a climate of peace and security which can be achieved through the joint effort of all States in promoting the reduction of international tension and in developing international cooperation in a spirit of friendship, respect for human rights and understanding among all States,

Convinced that world tourism can be a vital force for world peace and can provide the moral and intellectual basis for international understanding and interdependence,

Convinced further that world tourism can contribute to the establishment of a new international economic order that will help to eliminate the widening economic gap between developed and developing countries and ensure the steady acceleration of economic and social development and progress, in particular of the developing countries,

Aware that world tourism can only flourish if based on equity, sovereign equality, non-interference in internal affairs and cooperation among all States, irrespective of their economic and social systems, and if its ultimate aim is the improvement of the quality of life and the creation of better living conditions for all peoples, worthy of human dignity,

Agrees, in this spirit, to declare the following:

1. Tourism is considered an activity essential to the life of nations because of its direct effects on the social, cultural, educational and economic sectors of national societies and their international relations. Its development is

163

linked to the social and economic development of nations and can only be possible if man has access to creative rest and holidays and enjoys the freedom to travel within the framework of free time and leisure whose profoundly human character it underlines. Its very existence and development depend entirely on the existence of a state of lasting peace, to which tourism itself is required to contribute.

2. On the threshold of the twenty-first century and in view of the problems facing mankind, it seems timely and necessary to analyse the phenomenon of tourism, in relation fundamentally to the dimensions it has assumed since the granting to workers of the right to annual paid holidays moved tourism from a restricted elitist activity to a wider activity integrated into social and economic life.

3. As a result of peoples' aspirations to tourism, the initiatives taken by States regarding legislation and institutions, the permanent activities of voluntary bodies representing the various strata of the population and the technical contribution made by specialized professionals, modern tourism has come to play an important role within the range of human activities. States have recognized this fact and the great majority of them have entrusted the World Tourism Organization with the task of ensuring the harmonious and sustained development of tourism, in cooperation, in appropriate cases, with the Specialized Agencies of the United Nations and the other international organizations concerned.

4. The right to use of leisure, and in particular the right to access to holidays and to freedom of travel and tourism, a natural consequence of the right to work, is recognized as an aspect of the fulfilment of the human being by the Universal Declaration of Human Rights as well as by the legislation of many States. It entails for society the duty of providing for its citizens the best practical, effective and non-discriminatory access to this type of activity. Such an effort must be in harmony with the priorities, institutions and traditions of each individual country.

5. There are many constraints on the development of tourism. Nation and groups of nations should determine and study these constraints, and adopt measures aimed at attenuating their negative influence.

6. The share tourism represents in national economies and in international trade makes it a significant factor in world development. Its consistent major role in national economic activity, in international transactions and in securing balance of payments equilibrium makes it one of the main activities of the world economy.

7. Within each country, domestic tourism contributes to an improved balance of the national economy through a redistribution of the national income. Domestic tourism also heightens the awareness of common interest and contributes to the development of activities favourable to the general economy of the country. Thus, the development of tourism from abroad should be accompanied by a similar effort to expand domestic tourism.

8. The economic returns of tourism, however real and significant they may be, do not and cannot constitute the only criterion for the decision by States to encourage this activity. The right to holidays, the opportunity for the citizen to get to know his own environment, a deeper awareness of his national identity and of the solidarity that links him to his compatriots and the sense of belonging to a culture and to a people are all major reasons for stimulating the individual's participation in domestic and international tourism, through access to holidays and travel.

9. The importance that millions of our contemporaries attach to tourism in the use of their free time and in their concept of the quality of life makes it a need that governments should take into account and support.

10. Social tourism is an objective which society must pursue in the interest of those citizens who are least privileged in the exercise of their right to rest.

11. Through its effects on the physical and mental health of individuals practising it, tourism is a factor that favours social stability, improves the working capacity of communities and promotes individual as well as collective well-being.

12. Through the wide range of services needed to satisfy its requirements, tourism creates new activities of considerable importance which are a source of new employment. In this respect, tourism constitutes a positive element for social development in all the countries where it is practised irrespective of their level of development.

13. With respect to international relations and the search for peace, based on justice and respect of individual and national aspirations, tourism stands out as a positive and ever-present factor in promoting mutual knowledge and understanding and as a basis for reaching a greater level of respect and confidence among all the peoples of the world.

14. Modern tourism results from the adoption of a social policy which led to the workers gaining annual paid holidays and represents the recognition of a fundamental right of the human being to rest and leisure. It has become a factor contributing to social stability, mutual understanding among individuals and peoples and individual betterment. In addition to its well-known economic aspects, it has acquired a cultural and moral dimension which must be fostered and protected against the harmful distortions which can be brought about by economic factors. Public authorities and the travel trade should accordingly participate in development of tourism by formulating guidelines aimed at encouraging appropriate investments.

15. Youth tourism requires the most active attention since young people have less adequate income than others for travelling or taking holidays. A positive policy should provide youth with the utmost encouragement and facilities. The same attention should be provided for the elderly and handicapped.

16. In the universal efforts to establish a new international economic order, tourism can, under appropriate conditions, play a positive role in furthering equilibrium, cooperation, mutual understanding and solidarity among all countries.

17. Nations should promote improved conditions of employment for workers engaged in tourism and confirm and protect their right to establish professional trade unions and collective bargaining.

18. Tourism resources available in the various countries consist at the same time of space, facilities and values. These are resources whose use cannot be left uncontrolled without running the risk of their deterioration, or even their destruction. The satisfaction of tourism requirements must not be prejudicial to the social and economic interests of the population in tourist areas, to the environment or, above all, to natural resources, which are the fundamental attraction of tourism, and historical and cultural sites. All tourism resources are part of the heritage of mankind. National communities and the entire international community must take the necessary steps to ensure their preservation. The conservation of historical, cultural and religious sites represents at all times, and notably in time of conflict, one of the fundamental responsibilities of States.

19. International cooperation in the field of tourism is an endeavour in which the characteristics of peoples and basic interests of individual States must be respected. In this field, the central and decisive role of the World Tourism Organization as a conceptualizing and harmonizing body is obvious.

20. Bilateral and multilateral technical and financial cooperation cannot be looked upon as an act of assistance since it constitutes the pooling of the means necessary for the utilization of resources for the benefit of all parties.

21. In the practice of tourism, spiritual elements must take precedence over technical and material elements. The spiritual elements are essentially as follows:

    a) the total fulfilment of the human being,

    b) a constantly increasing contribution to education,

    c) equality of destiny of nations,

    d) the liberation of man in a spirit of respect for his identity and dignity,

    e) the affirmation of the originality of cultures and respect for the moral heritage of peoples.

22. Preparation for tourism should be integrated with the training of the citizen for his civic responsibilities. In this respect, governments should mobilize the means of education and information at their disposal and should facilitate the work of individuals and bodies involved in this en-

deavour. Preparation for tourism, for holidays and for travel could usefully form part of the process of youth education and training. For these reasons, the integration of tourism into youth education constitutes a basic element favourable to the permanent strengthening of peace.

23. Any long-term analysis of mankind's social, cultural and economic development should take due account of national and international tourist and recreational activities. These activities now form an integral part of the life of modern national and international societies. Bearing in mind the acknowledged values of tourism which are inseparble from it, the authorities will have to give more increased attention to the development of national and international tourist and recreational activity, based on an ever-wider participation of peoples in holidays and travel as well as the movement of persons for numerous other purposes, with a view to ensuring the orderly growth of tourism in a manner consistent with the other basic needs of society.

24. The States and other participants in the Conference, together with the World Tourism Organization, are strongly urged to take into account the guidelines, viewpoints and recommendations emanating from the Conference so that they can contribute, on the basis of their experience and in the context of their day-to-day activities to the practical implementation of the objectives set with a view to broadening the process of development of world tourism and breathing new life into it.

25. The Conference urges the World Tourism Organization to take all necessary measures, through its own internal machinery and, where appropriate, in cooperation with other international, intergovernmental and non-governmental bodies, so as to permit the global implementation of the principles, concepts and guidelines contained in this final document.

APPENDIX J

TOURISM BILL OF RIGHTS AND
TOURIST CODE ADOPTED IN SOFIA

After several years of concertation and negotiation, the Tourism Bill of Rights and Tourist Code, which were examined in depth at the fourth and fifth sessions of the WTO General Assembly in Rome and New Delhi, have just been adopted by the Sixth Assembly in Sofia.

The principles set forth in the text of the Tourism Bill of Rights and Tourist Code fulfil the rightful expectations of private and official travel and tourism circles.

In its resolution the General Assembly recommended that States see to it that all interested parties put into practice the principles of these texts insofar as is possible without prejudice to existing legislation and regulations.

Aware of the importance of tourism in the life of peoples because of its direct and positive effects on the social, economic, cultural and educational sectors or national society and the contribution it can make, in the spirit of the United Nations Charter and the Manila Declaration on World Tourism, to improving mutual understanding, bringing peoples closer together and, consequently, strengthening international cooperation,

Recalling that, as recognized by the General Assembly of the United Nations, the World Tourism Organization has a central and decisive role in the development of tourism with a view to contributing, in accordance with Article 3, paragraph 1 of its Statutes, *"to economic development, international understanding, peace, prosperity and universal respect for, and observation of, human rights and fundamental freedoms for all without distinction as to race, sex, language or religion",*

Recalling the Universal Declaration of Human rights adopted by the General Assembly of the United Nations on 10 December 1948, and in particular Article 24 which provides that *"Everyone has the right to rest and leisure, including reasonable limitation of working hours and periodic holidays with pay",* as well as the International Covenant on Economic, Social and Cultural Rights adopted by the General Assembly of the United Nations on 16 December 1966, which invites States to ensure for everyone *"Rest, leisure and reasonable limitation of working hours and periodic holidays with pay, as well as remuneration for public holidays",*

Considering the resolution and recommendations adopted by the United Nations Conference on International Travel and Tourism (Rome, September 1963), and particularly those aimed at promoting tourism development in the various countries and at simplifying government formalities in respect of international travel,

Drawing its inspiration from the principles set forth in the Manila Declaration on World Tourism adopted by the World Tourism Conference on 10 October 1980, which emphasizes the true, human dimension of tourism, recognizes the new role of tourism as an appropriate instrument for improving the quality of life of all peoples and a vital force for peace and international understanding and defines the responsibility of States for developing tourism and, in particular, for fostering awareness of tourism among the peoples of the world and protecting and enhancing the tourism resources which are part of mankind's heritage, with a view to contributing to the establishment of a new international economic order,

Solemnly affirming, as a natural consequence of the right to work, the fundamental right of everyone, as already sanctioned by the Universal Declaration of Human Rights, to rest, leisure and periodic holidays with pay and to use them for holiday purposes, to travel freely for education and pleasure and to enjoy the advantages of tourism, both within his country of residence and abroad,

Invites the States to draw inspiration from the principles set forth below constituting the Tourism Bill of Rights and Tourist Code, and to apply them in accordance with the precedures prescribed in the legislation and regulations of their own countries.

TOURISM BILL OF RIGHTS
Article I

The right of everyone to rest and leisure, reasonable limitation of working hours, periodic leave with pay and freedom to travel without limitation, within the bounds of the law, is universally recognized.

The exercise of this right constitutes a factor of social balance and enhancement of national and universal awareness.

Article II

As a consequence of this right, the States should formulate and implement policies aimed at promoting the harmonious development of domestic and international tourism and leisure activities for the benefit of all those taking part in them.

Article III

To this end the States should:

  a) *encourage the orderly and harmonious growth of both domestic and international tourism;*

  b) *integrate their tourism policies with their overall development policies at all levels—local, regional, national and international—and broaden tourism cooperation within both a bilateral and multilateral framework, including that of the World Tourism Organization;*

c) *give due attention to the principles of the Manila Declaration and the Acapulco Document on World Tourism "while formulating and implementing, as appropriate, their tourism policies, plans and programmes, in accordance with their national priorities and within the framework of the programme of work of the World Tourism Organization";*

d) *encourage the adoption of measures enabling everyone to participate in domestic and international tourism, especially by a better allocation of work and leisure time, the establishment or improvement of systems of annual leave with pay, the staggering of holiday dates and by particular attention to tourism for the young, elderly and disabled; and*

e) *in the interest of present and future generations, protect the tourism environment which, being at once human, natural, social and cultural, is the legacy of all mankind.*

Article IV

The States should also:

a) *encourage the access of domestic and international tourists to the heritage of the host communities by applying the provisions of existing facilitation instruments issuing from the United Nations, the International Civil Aviation Organization, the International Maritime Organization, the Customs Cooperation Council or from any other body, the World Tourism Organization in particular, with a view to increasingly liberalizing travel;*

b) *promote tourism awareness and facilitate contact between visitors and host communities with a view to their mutual understanding and betterment;*

c) *ensure the safety of visitors and the security of their belongings through preventive and protective measures;*

d) *afford the best possible conditions of hygiene and access to health services as well as of the prevention of communicable diseases and accidents;*

e) *prevent any possibility of using tourism to exploit others for prostitution purposes; and*

f) *reinforce, for the protection of tourists and the population of the host community, measures to prevent the illegal use of narcotics.*

Article V

The States should lastly:

a) *permit domestic and international tourists to move freely about the country, without prejudice to any limitative measures taken in the national interest concerning certain areas of the territory;*

b) *not allow any discriminatory measures in regard to tourists;*

c) *allow tourists prompt access to administrative and legal services and to consular representatives, and make available internal and external public communications; and*

d) *contribute to the information of tourists with a view to fostering understanding of the customs of the populations constituting the host communities at places of transit and sojourn.*

Article VI

The populations constituting the host communities in places of transit and sojourn are entitled to free access to their own tourism resources while fostering respect, through their attitude and behaviour, for their natural and cultural environment.

They are also entitled to expect from tourists understanding of the respect for their customs, religions and other elements of their cultures which are part of the human heritage.

To facilitate such understanding and respect, the dissemination of appropriate information should be encouraged on:

a) *the customs of host communities, their traditional and religious practices, local taboos and sacred sites and shrines which must be respected;*

b) *their artistic, archaeological and cultural treasures which must be preserved; and*

c) *wildlife and other natural resources which must be protected.*

Article VII

The populations constituting the host communities in places of transit and sojourn are invited to receive tourists with the greatest possible hospitality, courtesy and respect necessary for the development of harmonious human and social relations.

Article VIII

Tourism professionals and suppliers of tourism and travel services can make a positive contribution to tourism development and to implementation of the provisions of this Bill of Rights.

They should conform to the principles of this Bill of Rights and honour commitments of any kind entered into within the context of their professional activities, ensuring the provisions of quality products so as to help affirm the humanist nature of tourism.

They should in particular refrain from encouraging the use of tourism for all forms of exploitation of others.

Article IX

Encouragement should be given to tourism professionals and suppliers of tourism and travel services by granting them, through appropriate national and international legislation the necessary facilities to enable them to:

a) *exercise their activities in favourable conditions, free from any particular impediment or discrimination;*

b) *benefit from general and technical training schemes, both within their countries and abroad, so as to ensure the availability of skilled manpower; and*

c) *cooperate among themselves as well as with the public authorities, through national and international organizations, with a view to improving the coordination of their services and the quality of their services.*

TOURIST CODE

Article X

Tourists should, by their behaviour, foster understanding and friendly relations among peoples, at both the national and international levels, and thus contribute to lasting peace.

Article XI

At places of transit and sojourn tourists must respect the established political, social, moral and religious order and comply with the legislation and regulations in force.

In these places tourists must also:

a) *show the greatest understanding for the customs, beliefs and behaviour of the host communities and the greatest respect for their natural and cultural heritage;*

b) *refrain from accentuating the economic, social and cultural differences between themselves and the local population;*

c) *be receptive to the culture of the host communities, which is an integral part of the common human heritage; and*

d) *refrain from exploiting others for prostitution purposes;*

e) *refrain from trafficking, carrying or the use of narcotics and/or other prohibited drugs.*

Article XII

During their travel from one country to another and within the host country tourists should be able, by appropriate government measures, to benefit from:

a) *relaxation of administrative and financial controls; and*

b) *the best possible conditions of transport and sojourn that can be offered by suppliers of tourism services.*

Article XIII

Tourists should be afforded free access, both within and outside their countries, to sites and places of tourist interest and, subject to existing regulations and limitations, to move about freely in places of transit and sojourn.

On access to sites and places of tourist interest and throughout their transit and sojourn, tourists should be able to benefit from:

a) *objective, precise and complete information on conditions and facilities provided during their travel and sojourn by official tourism bodies and suppliers of tourism services;*

b) *safety of their persons, security of their belongings and protection of their rights as consumers;*

c) *satisfactory public hygiene, particularly so far as accommodation, catering and transport are concerned, information on the effective prevention of communicable diseases and accidents and ready access to health services;*

d) *access to swift and efficient public communications, both internal and external;*

e) *administrative and legal procedures and guarantees necessary for the protection of their rights; and*

f) *the practice of their own religion and the use of existing facilities for that purpose.*

Article XIV

Everyone is entitled to make his needs known to legislative representatives and public authorities so that he may exercise his right to rest and leisure in order to enjoy the benefits or tourism under the most favourable conditions and, where appropriate and to the extent consistent with law, associate with others for that purpose.

APPENDIX K

THE HAGUE DECLARATION ON TOURISM

The Inter-Parliamentary Conference on Tourism,

Organized at the Hague (Netherlands) from 10 to 14 April 1989 jointly by the Inter-Parliamentary Union (IPU)* and the World Tourism Organization (WTO)**, at the invitation of the Netherlands Inter-Parliamentary Group,

Considering that it is in the interest of all countries to facilitate both individual and group tourist travel, visits and stays which, contributing as they do to economic, social and cultural development, foster the creation of a climate of confidence and mutual understanding between the States members of the international community, the development of international co-operation and, hence, lasting peace in the world,

Considering that, in so doing, account should also be taken of the special problems of the developing countries in the field of tourism,

Recalling the Universal Declaration of Human Rights adopted by the General Assembly of the United Nations on 10 Dcember 1948, and in particular its Article 24, which states: "Everyone has the right to rest and leisure, including reasonable limitation of working hours and periodic holidays with pay", as well as Article 7 of the International Covenant on Economic, Social and Cultural Rights, adopted by the General Assembly of the United Nations on 16 December 1966, by which States undertake to ensure, for everyone, "Rest, leisure, reasonable limitation of working hours and periodic holidays with pay, as well as remuneration for public holidays", and Article 12 of the International Covenant on Civil and Political Rights, also adopted on 16 December 1966 by the General Assembly of the United Nations, which states: "Everyone shall be free to leave any country, including his own,"

Considering the resolution and recommendations adopted by the United Nations Conference on International Travel and Tourism (Rome, September 1963) and, in particular, those concerning the promotion of tourism development in the various countries of the world and the simplification of governmental formalities for international travel,

Inspired by the principles set forth in the Manila Declaration on World Tourism, and the Acapulco Document, the Tourist Code and Tourism Bill of Rights, underscoring the human dimension of tourism, recognizing the new role of tourism as an instrument for improving the quality of life of all peoples

*The worldwide organization of Parliaments in which 112 national Parliaments and the European Parliament are at present represented. The IPU was founded in 1889.
**An intergovernmental organization of universal character created in 1975 with the aim of promoting and developing domestic and international tourism.

and as a vital force for peace and international understanding, and defining the responsibilities of the State in its development, particularly with respect to promoting awareness about the importance of tourism among the peoples of the world and protecting and enhancing tourism resources as part of the heritage of mankind, with a view to contributing to the establishment of a more just and equitable new international economic order,

Recalling the "central and decisive role" of the World Tourism Organization (WTO) in the development of tourism as recognized by the General Assembly of the United Nations, with a view "to contributing to economic development, international understanding, peace, prosperity and universal respect for, and observance of, human rights and fundamental freedoms for all without distinction as to race, sex, language or religion"*,

Aware that an important contribution to the harmonious development of tourism can be made by the work of numerous inter-governmental and non-governmental organizations, such as the International Labour Organisation (ILO), the World Health Organization (WHO), the United Nations Educational, Scientific and Cultural Organization (UNESCO), the International Maritime Organization (IMO), the International Civil Aviation Organization (ICAO), the United Nations Environment Programme (UNEP), the International Criminal Police Organization (ICPO-INTERPOL), and the Organisation for Economic Co-operation and Development (OECD), and *stressing* the importance of close co-operation between those organizations and WTO,

Solemnly affirming, as a natural conseqence of the right to work, the fundamental right, already consecrated in the Universal Declaration of Human Rights, the Covenants on Human Rights of the United Nations and in other universal and regional legal instruments, of everyone to rest, leisure and periodic leave with pay, and the right to use such time for the purposes of holidays, to travel freely for education of pleasure and to enjoy the benefits of tourism, both within his country of residence and abroad,

Recalling that it was at The Hague that the First International Congress of Official Tourist Traffic Associations met in 1925 and founded the International Union of Official Travel Organizations, which in 1975 was transformed into the World Tourism Organization,

Pronounces The Hague Declaration on Tourism as an instrument of international co-operation, rapprochement between peoples and as a factor of individual and collective development,

Urges Parliaments, Governments, public and private authorities, organizations, associations and institutions responsible for tourism activities, tourism professionals, as well as tourists themselves, to consider carefully and draw constant inspiration from its principles, as set forth below:

*Article 3(1) of the WTO Statutes.

PRINCIPLE I

1. Tourism has become a phenomenon of every-day life for hundreds of millions of people today:

    a) It encompasses all free movements of persons away from their places of residence and work, as well as the service industries created to satisfy the needs resulting from these movements;

    b) It constitutes an activity essential to the lives of human beings and modern societies, having become an important form of using the free time of individuals and the main vehicle for interpersonal relations and political, economic and cultural contact made necessary by the internationalization of all sectors of the life of nations;

    c) It should be the concern of everyone. It is both a consequence and a decisive factor of the quality of life in contemporary society. Therefore, Parliaments and Governments should accord increasingly sustained attention to tourism with a view to ensuring its development in harmony with the other fundamental needs and activities of societies.

2. All Governments should work for national, regional and international peace and security which are essential to the development of domestic and international tourism.

PRINCIPLE II

1. Tourism can be an effective instrument for socio-economic growth for all countries, if at the same time the necessary measures are taken to tackle the more urgent national priorities and to allow the national economy to reach an acceptable level of self-sufficiency in which the country does not have to spend in excess of what it can hope to earn from tourism.

2. Consequently, the following measures should in particular be taken, if necessary with the help of the various forms of bilateral and multilateral technical co-operation, to ensure:

    a) That a sound infrastructure is built up and the basic facilities are provided;

    b) That training institutes are set up to meet the personnel needs of the tourism industry at different levels;

    c) That tourism forms part of an integrated plan for development of the country in which agriculture, industrial development, medical care, social welfare, education, etc. are other priority sectors;

    d) That the development of domestic tourism be equally encouraged with the promotion of international tourism. A strong base of domestic tourism will be a big asset for the development of international tourism in the country;

e) That even in planning for domestic tourism, the Master Plan approach on an area basis is developed to bring about a balanced and integrated growth for the benefit of the community; and

f) That the overall capacity of the natural, physical and cultural environment of destinations to receive tourism (carrying capacity) be always carefully taken into consideration.

PRINCIPLE III

1. An unspoilt natural, cultural and human environment is a fundamental condition for the development of tourism. Moreover, rational management of tourism may contribute significantly to the protection and development of the physical environment and the cultural heritage, as well as to improving the quality of life.

2. In view of this intrinsic inter-relationship between tourism and environment, effective measures should be taken to:

    a) Inform and educate tourists, both domestic and international, to preserve, conserve and respect the natural, cultural and human environment in places they visit;

    b) Promote the integrated planning of tourism development on the basis of the concept of "sustainable development" which was set forth in the Report of the World Commission of Enviroment and Development (Brundtland Report) and in the report "The Environmental Perspective to the Year 2000 and Beyond" of the United Nations Environment Programme (UNEP), both of which documents have been approved by the UN General Assembly;

    c) Determine and ensure respect for carrying-capacity levels of sites visited by tourists even if this implies restricting access to such sites at certain periods or seasons;

    d) Continue to compile an inventory of man-made and/or natural tourist sites of recreational, sporting, historical, archaeological, artistic, cultural, religious, scientific, social or technical interest and ensure that tourism development plans take special account of aspects related with environmental protection and the need to promote awareness among tourists, the tourism industry and the public at large of the importance of safeguarding the natural and cultural environment;

    e) Encourage development of alternative forms of tourism which favour closer contact and understanding between tourists and receiving populations, preserve cultural identity and offer distinctive and original tourist products and facilities;

    f) Ensure the necessary co-operation between the public and private sector to this end both at national and international levels.

PRINCIPLE IV

1. In view of the eminently human character of tourism, consideration should always be given to the specific problems of tourists themselves, whether they be domestic or international. An international tourist is any person:

   a) Who intends to travel, and/or travels, to a country other than that in which he or she has his or her usual place of residence, and

   b) Whose main purpose of travel is a visit or stay not exceeding three months, unless a stay longer than three months is authorized or the three months authorization is renewed, and

   c) Who will not exercise, whether or not he or she is called upon to exercise, any activity remunerated in the country visited, and

   d) Who, at the end of the said visit or stay, will obligatorily leave the country visited, either to return to the country where he or she has his or her usual place of residence or to travel to another country.

2. It logically follows that a person cannot be considered an international tourist if he or she does not fulfil all the conditions enumerated in paragraph 1 and, in particular, if, after entering the country as a tourist for a tourist visit or stay, he or she seeks to prolong his or her length of visit or stay so as to establish residence and/or to exercise a remunerated activity there.

PRINCIPLE V

1. The right of everyone to rest and leisure, including reasonable limitation of working hours and periodic holidays with pay, and the right to travel freely, subject to reasonable restrictions which are explicitly provided for by law and which do not call into question the principle of the freedom of movement itself, must be universally recognized.

2. In order for these fundamental rights of every man and woman to be fully ensured, it is necessary to:

   a) Formulate and apply policies to promote harmonious development of domestic and international tourism and leisure activities for the benefit of all those who participate in them;

   b) Give due consideration to the principles set forth in the Manila Declaration on World Tourism, the Acapulco Document and the Tourism Bill of Rights and Tourist Code, particularly when States formulate or apply tourism development policies, plans and programmes in accordance with their national priorities.

PRINCIPLE VI

The promotion of tourism requires facilitation of travel. Effective measures should therefore be taken by the public and private sectors to:

a) Facilitate tourist travel, visits and stays, both on an individual and collective basis, irrespective of the mode of transport used;

b) Contribute effectively to the expansion of tourist travel, visits and stays by taking appropriate facilitation measures with respect to passports, visas, health and exchange controls and the status of tourism representations abroad;

c) Foster, to this end, the adoption and implementation of the Budapest Convention to Facilitate Tourist Travel, Visits and Stays, thereby permitting the liberalization of legal provisions applicable to tourists and the harmonization of technical standards concerning the operation of tourism enterprises, travel agencies and other bodies serving tourists.

PRINCIPLE VII

The safety, security and protection of tourists and respect for their dignity are a precondition to develop tourism. Therefore, it is indispensable:

a) That the measures to facilitate tourist travel, visit and stays be accompanied by measures to ensure the safety, security and protection of tourists and tourist facilities and the dignity of tourists;

b) That an effective policy concerning the safety, security and protection of tourists and tourist facilities and respect for the dignity of tourists be established for this purpose;

c) To identify precisely the tourist goods, facilities and equipment which, because of their use by tourists, require special attention;

d) To prepare and make available appropriate documentation and information in cases of threats to tourist facilities and/or tourist sites;

e) To implement, in accordance with the procedures specific to the systems of law of each country, legal provisions in the field of tourist protection, including in particular the ability for tourists to seek effective legal remedy from the national courts in the event of acts harmful to their persons, or property, and in particular the most grievous acts, such as terrorism;

f) That States co-operate within WTO to prepare a catalogue of recommended measures governing the safety, security and protection of tourists.

PRINCIPLE VIII

Terrorism constitutes a real threat for tourism and tourist movements. Terrorists must be treated like any other criminals and should be pursued and punished without statutory limitation, no country thus being a safe haven for terrorists.

PRINCIPLE IX

1. The quality of tourism as a person-to-person business depends on the quality of the personal service provided. Therefore appropriate education for the general public starting at the school level, education and training of tourism professionals and the preparation of new entrants in the profession are essential for the tourist industry and the development of tourism.

2. To this end, effective measures should be taken to:

    a) Prepare individuals for travel and tourism, in particular by including tourism in school and university curricula;

    b) Enhance the status of tourist professions and encourage young people in particular to embark upon a career in tourism;

    c) Establish a network of institutions capable of providing not only training but also education in tourism on the basis of an internationally standardized curriculum which would also facilitate mutual recognition of qualifications and exchanges of tourism personnel;

    d) Promote, in accordance with the recommendations of UNESCO in this field, training of trainers, permanent education and refresher courses for all tourism personnel or teachers regardless of level;

    e) Recognize the vital role of the mass media in developing tourism.

PRINCIPLE X

1. Tourism should be planned on an integrated and coherent basis by public authorities, and between them and industry, taking into consideration all aspects of this complex phenomenon.

2. Whereas tourism has in the life of nations industrial importance at least equal to that of other economic and social activities, and whereas the role of tourism will expand in step with a scientific and technical progress and increases in free time, it appears necessary to strengthen, in all countries, the powers and responsibilities of the national tourism administrations, according them the same rank as administrations responsible for other major economic sectors.

3. The need for a global approach to the problems raised by tourism requires the establishment of a genuine national tourism policy, in whose formulation Parliaments, when properly equipped, can play a special role so as to be in a position to adopt specific legislation on tourism and, if required, an authentic Tourism Code.

4. Recognizing the international dimensions of tourism, worldwide as well as regional, international co-operation is essential for its harmonious development through direct inter-State co-operation and through the channel of international organizations, such as WTO, and between the different

components of the private sector of tourism through non-governmental and professional organizations.

The Inter-Parliamentary Conference on Tourism,

Also approves the Specific Conclusions and Recommendations contained in the Annex.

SPECIFIC CONCLUSIONS AND RECOMMENDATIONS

The Inter-Parliamentary Conference on Tourism,

Having set out the principles contained in The Hague Declaration on Tourism,

Adopts the following specific Conclusions and Recommendations.

I.
THE PLACE OF TOURISM IN ECONOMIC AND SOCIAL DEVELOPMENT
Conclusions

1. The present importance of tourism and its economic future potential are indicated by the following statistics (referring to 1988):

    ● Total expenditure on domestic and international tourism (including air fares) is estimated to represent 12 per cent of total world GNP.

    ● Some 1.5 billion domestic and international tourist trips were made involving one-third of the world's population.

    ● International tourism accounted for 6 per cent of total world exports and 25–30 per cent of world trade in services.

    ● International tourism is forecast to increase at an annual rate of approximately 4 per cent up to the year 2000, by which time it will be the world's largest export industry.

2. The potential impact of this dramatic growth on the economy, environment and people is of such magnitude that it may be referred to as the "Tourism Revolution."

3. Tourism is the way in which the individual can savour the unknown, acquire understanding and experience the world in its fullness; it is a revolution which enables all citizens of the world to travel, and one in which they can be wholeheartedly proud to participate.

4. Tourism stands out as a positive and ever-present factor in promoting mutual knowledge and understanding, and therefore peace and détente; conversely, tourism is strongly hampered by tension and conflicts and always fostered by peace.

5. Adequate leisure is a social necessity, but can become a burden if not put to proper use; among the many possibilities of spending spare time, not one (with the possible exception of television) has achieved such importance as tourism.

6. The economic potential for tourism development is almost unlimited; however, considerable investment and expenditure will be required.

7. Tourism expenditures, in addition to producing direct revenues, percolate down through many levels of the economy, creating not only direct but also indirect employment, foreign exchange earnings, State revenue, patronage of craftsmen and artists and development of regions with no other commercial or industrial base.

8. At present, the share of developing countries in worldwide tourism revenues is comparatively small; however, the developing countries are in a position to reap more benefits from international tourism, but should never lose sight of the fact that the benefits should not be sought at any cost.

9. Domestic tourism trips and expenditure, and therefore their contribution to economic wealth and employment at national, regional and local levels, are already a very large proportion of total worldwide tourism. Furthermore, the development and facilitation of domestic tourism is an important contributor to the enhancement of social contacts and understanding between people.

10. The development of domestic tourism also creates a basic tourist infrastructre and manpower skills which will assist countries in developing and harmoniously integrating an international tourism industry.

11. Tourism is a smokeless industry and is not necessarily accompanied by the devastating consequences that often come with industrialization; there are however potential dangers to both the physical and cultural environments which require the attention of States.

12. Well-preserved monuments, vital living traditions and a pristine natural environment will attract tourists and encourage them to return again; the expenditures of these tourists will in turn provide an economic motivation for the preservation of a nation's culture and environment. On the other hand, if such monuments and the environment are not well preserved, tourists will no longer be attracted and the economic benefits of tourism will diminish.

13. If uncontrolled and unplanned, tourism growth can lead to negative social, cultural and economic friction between tourist visitors and the local population, and to a uniform type of tourist behavior and requirements which in the long term could have an adverse impact on the cultural diversity and identity of local populations in the receiving countries.

14. The present pattern of worldwide tourism demand is very seasonal and highly concentrated in certain months of the year. This is not only due to climatic and motivational factors on the part of tourists, but is also caused by current industrial practices and national legislation governing annual factory closures and paid annual leave for employees, coupled with the calendar of school holiday dates.

15. The tourism industry has failed to present the real image of tourism and, at least until now, has not been successful in developing effective support for tourism particularly from parliamentarians.

16. The national tourism industries in most destination countries are highly fragmented, consisting of small-scale, individually operated and under-capitalized tourism enterprises. While this can satisfy the diverse and individualistic needs of tourists, there is a growing imbalance between these and the increasingly concentrated nature of international tourism supply (international tour operators, airlines and hoteliers).

17. Due to international competition, the costs of promoting tourism indus-tries are increasing, both in developing countries and "mature" economies (where tourism is increasingly seen as one of the solutions to regional development). There is also a need to measure the effectiveness of national, regional and local tourism promotion policies conducted by or together with the public sector.

18. It is essential for public authorities at all levels in all countries, especially Parliaments, to take an active role in creating favourable conditions for tourism, and, in particular, to provide the financial and other means for comprehensive information programmes about tourism.

19. The present and future development of tourism demands more active Government support for information and promotion of tourism as well as provision of infrastructure; new markets need to be developed and steps should be taken to ensure co-operation in all spheres—public and private—in the best interest of stimulating the tourist sector.

Recommendations

20. Tourism should be planned on an integral basis taking into account all aspects of legislation relating to other sectors such as transport, employ-ment, health, agriculture, communications, etc.

21. The overall role of parliamentarians, through legislation, should be to analyse, co-ordinate, facilitate and regulate both domestic and in-ternational tourism development within the context of their national de-velopment priorities.

22. Countries should determine their national priorities and tourism's role in the "hierarchy" of these priorities as well as the optimum tourism strategy, within these priorities. This strategy should define, among others, the balance to be sought between international and domestic tourism, and take into account the carrying capacity of destinations and the roles of state, regional and local organizations.

23. Within the overall national tourism strategy, priority attention should be given to selective and controlled development of tourist infrastructure, facilities, demand, and overall tourist capacity, in order to protect the environment, and local population, so as to avoid any negative impacts

which unplanned tourism might produce. In tourism planning and area development it is essential for States to strike a harmonious balance between economic and ecological considerations.

24. National and transnational corporations should be required by law to take adequate preventive measures to avoid damage to the environment and tourist sites; these corporations should be properly called to account in the event of their causing damage as well as be obliged to take all measures to reduce the consequences and repair such damage.

25. Dangerous industrial practices, particularly the transport, treatment and storage of toxic and radioactive substances and waste, should be subject to strict legal controls, and the dumping of such waste made illegal, so as to avoid damage to the natural and human environment. National and transnational corporations that are the source of such damage should be obliged to assume responsibility for it and to repair it.

26. Research and back-up are essential to develop a country's tourism potential effectively and with maximum benefits; this requires parallel enhancement of the status of the tourism administrations of each State— which does not imply that the State need exercise an interventionist role in tourism—rather it should ensure that the tourism industry has the maximum opportunity to exercise its functions.

27. As tourism infrastructure is created, it is absolutely essential that general tourism education for the population as a whole, particularly in schools, as well as specialized training for tourism professionals, be developed at the national level; major goals should be the establishment of tourism as a respected profession and tourism consciousness on the part of the population.

28. All tourist-generating countries should more effectively stagger their industrial and school holidays in order to reduce the harmful effects of the over-seasonal nature of tourism demand (over-crowding and delays at airports, frontier crossings, etc.) and the associated negative effects these have on tourist employment, tourist facilitation and security (health, exploitation).

29. Governments should provide the basic infrastructure for tourism development and take special support measures for "infant" tourism industries, especially small enterprises and in development regions. This support may take the form of direct investment, financial incentives to private investment, and expenditure on promotion.

30. In a country wich is not self-sufficient in many areas and which does not have a tourist infrastructure already in place, it is vital for costs to be weighed against prospective earnings from tourism, and the entire equation then viewed in the light of national priorities. All efforts should be made to ensure that destination countries receive the maximum share of receipts from tourist activities. This implies that countries should optimize

tourism development strategies in order to make the greatest possible use of local facilities and resources.

31. Special assistance, which need not be financial, should be given by developed countries to developing countries; this could well take the form of encouraging their citizens to take their holidays in the developing countries.

32. Governments, national tourist organizations and private industry should make every effort to work together in providing the financing to bring tourism to its full fruition and enable all people to reap its benefits.

33. Great stress must be placed on the promotion of tourism by industry, with the support of Governments, in terms of both financing and encouragement. Such support can contribute to economic development and increased employment, while likewise ensuring a good infrastructure and protecting the environment as well as the cultural assets of each country. Therefore, all Governments together with the tourism industry should carry out active tourist policies to the benefit of their countries now and in the future.

34. States should assume the responsibility for devising ways of using tourism to develop new forms of patronage—thus enabling traditional cultural forms to retain their integrity, vigour and quality.

35. In a developing country just at the beginning of its tourism activity, it is essential that planning and implementation be co-ordinated at national level and all efforts should be made through international co-operation to benefit from the positive experiences and avoid the mistakes of other more developed tourist countries.

36. There are limits to the degree of decentralization and deconcentration that is possible in the tourism sector; at the very least, it implies the need for national machinery to ensure co-ordination of tourism policy between the national and the regional level of the State.

37. States should encourage the development of domestic tourism which is based on the right of the individual to holidays, offers each citizen the opportunity to get to know his or her own environment, to reaffirm national identity and to forge links of solidarity with compatriots, and helps each country to develop a basic tourism infrastructure.

38. Tourism legislation should be framed with three goals in view: (a) to protect the tourist, (b) to protect each country from the potential problems caused by tourism, particularly as regards environmental impact and cultural identity and (c) to promote tourism. In this respect, there is a need for close co-operation between the tourism industry and its specialists and the scientific bodies responsible for maintaining natural, man-made and cultural resources.

II.
THE FACILITATION OF TOURISM AND TOURIST TRAVEL, VISITS AND STAYS

Conclusions

39. The co-ordinated policies and actions by States to promote and encourage both individual and collective tourist travel, visits and stays may be termed facilitation.

40. As travel and tourism have grown rapidly in recent years, so the concept of facilitation has been refined and expanded: today it is customary to distinguish between two general groups of impediments to tourism: those that affect travellers in general (be they individuals or groups) and those that affect businesses providing services for tourists.

41. The process of eliminating impediments to travel in general is usually referred to simply as *facilitation* while the term *liberalization* is increasingly employed to denote the process of reducing barriers to business and trade in tourism services.

42. Facilitation has grown from its original narrow definition of a subject limited to frontier formalities and customs procedures. Today it is considered to be a matter of giving positive encouragement to travel and tourism, in particular by: adoption of measures enabling everyone to participate in domestic and international tourism, especially by a better allocation of work and leisure time, the establishment or improvement of systems of annual leave with pay and the staggering of holiday dates, and by particular attention to tourism for the young, elderly and disabled.

43. Historically, facilitation questions were addressed by States on a bilateral basis; subsequently, however, inter-governmental organizations came to be entrusted with facilitation questions affecting certain categories of travellers, modes of transport or type of tourist transaction; in this connection, special mention should be made of the texts adopted by the meetings of the following international organizations: the Chicago Convention of the International Civil Aviation Organization (1944), the Kyoto Convention of the Customs Co-operation Council (1973), the Convention on Facilitation of International Maritime Traffic of the International Maritime Organization (1965). Other international accords or documents of importance for facilitation include the Single European Act of the European Communities (1987), the International Health Regulations of the World Health Organization (1951), the Decision–Recommendation of the Council of the OECD on International Tourism Policy of 1985, various instruments adopted under the auspices of the International Labour Organization concerning Leave with Pay and the Final Act of the Conference on Security and Co-operation in Europe (Helsinki, 1976).

44. However, these instruments are incomplete as regards mode of transport, geographical coverage, and breadth of viewpoint.

45. Also there is a need for greater co-ordination and interaction between the different international organizations concerning facilitation and liberalization, and, more importantly, a global approach to tourism.

46. The most recent attempts to advance facilitation from the sectoral protection afforded by certain existing instruments to the universal coverage of all *bona fide* tourists regardless of mode of transport contemplated, are reflected in the draft Budapest Convention to Facilitate Tourist Travel, Visits and Stays.

47. Formalities affecting travellers in general are customarily grouped under the following headings:

    a) Passports and visas
    b) Currency and exchange controls
    c) Customs regulations
    d) Health formalities.

Passports and Visas
48. All documentation requirements may be considered obstacles to tourism when they are poorly administered, when applications are disapproved arbitrarily, when excessive fees are charged or when procedures are overly complicated or lengthy.

Currency and Exchange Controls
49. It should be recalled that currency and exchange controls not only affect the level of tourist expenditure but may also discourage travel to destinations practising such measures.

Customs Regulations
50. The main problem appears to be wide variations in duty-free allowances from country to country; declaration forms and customs inspections may also discourage tourist spending.

Health Formalities
51. Progress in combating disease is such that, according to the current International Health Regulations of the World Health Organization (WHO), the only certificate that should now be required is for vaccination against yellow fever.

52. The development of illicit trafficking in narcotic drugs and the growth of terrorism in recent years have both had a serious impact on facilitation.

53. While countries are obliged to deal with the growing problem of immigration flows (whether these are the result of economic and social imbalances between countries, or political situations), it must be recognized that restrictive legislation on immigration or discriminatory practices run counter to the facilitation of international tourism.

Recommendations

54. States should position tourism clearly within the framework of national priorities, and assess the impact of any legislation on the facilitation and liberalization of tourism to ensure that this does not impede flows of international tourism.

55. States should give increased attention to reconciling the seemingly opposed principles of facilitation and the security and protection of tourists and tourist amenities.

56. With a view to ensuring effective planning and co-ordination in all areas related to facilitation, States should adopt a national facilitation policy whose implementation shoul be entrusted, whenever possible, to National Facilitation Committees.

57. States should encourage tourism consciousness, that is, a welcoming attitude towards travellers and tourists, among customs and immigration officials, tourism personnel and the public at large, in order to respect human dignity and above all to avoid any discriminatory attitudes.

58. States should ensure that enhanced facilitation procedures are applied to special segments of the travelling community such as young people, the disabled and third-age tourists; such procedures might include, in particular, reduction or waiver of fees for issue of travel documents such as passports and visas, and fare reductions on public transport; in addition, States should adopt all necessary measures to facilitate the access of disabled people to tourist travel, visits and stays, irrespective of their special needs and requirements.

59. States should pay particular attention to the statistics forecasting the significant growth of international tourist traffic in the next several years, in order to ensure that they plan and develop passenger handling facilities and air traffic landing and take-off facilities and have them operational at the right time, so as not to hamper international air travel. In this respect the constructive work carried out to date by ICAO should be recognized and supported.

60. States should abide by the standards, regulations and information requirements of the WHO and, in particular, ensure that only the health certificate for vaccination against yellow fever is required—and only from a limited number of international travellers. WHO must receive an immediate update from Governments on changed health provisions in all countries.

61. With respect to AIDS, and in conformity with the position currently taken by the WHO member States, no discriminatory measures should be imposed on international tourists and travellers.

62. States should institute measures to ensure that tourists have easy access to emergency medical attention during their stay on the national territory.

63. Where possible and economic, developed States should liberalize policies to permit increased and more frequent air routes to and from developing countries in order to facilitate and accelerate traffic flows and facilitate tourists visits to these countries within short vacation periods.

64. Parliamentarians should lend their support to the current GATT initiative, in which WTO is involved, to liberalize trade in services, including tourism.

65. Parliamentarians should lend their support to the first comprehensive legal instrument dealing with facilitation of tourism regardless of mode of transport, namely the draft Budapest Convention to Facilitate Tourist Travel, Visits and Stays; they should also lend their support to the promotion, development and updating of existing legal instruments directly or indirectly concerned with the facilitation of tourist travel, visits and stays.

66. States should draw inspiration, in developing their national facilitation policy, from such principles as those adopted in 1989 at the Vienna follow-up meeting to the Conference on Security and Co-operation in Europe (CSCE).

III.
THE SECURITY AND PROTECTION OF TOURISTS, TOURIST SITES AND FACILITIES
Conclusions

67. In order to function properly and develop, tourism requires safety for travellers and holidaymakers be they national or international, and for their personal property, as well as safety and protection of tourist sites and facilities. This can be achieved by:

   a) The establishment and enforcement of safety standards for travel and tourist stays;

   b) Public information and education;

   c) Creation of the institutional framework to deal with safety problems of tourists in particular in emergencies; and

   d) International co-operation at bilateral, subregional, regional, interregional and global levels.

68. The security of tourists and their well-being and the maintenance of high quality standards in travel and tourist destinations cannot be seen in isolation from other public or national interests in particular those of the receiving country, and the environment in general. The interests of those who visit and receive must be mutually harmonized when developing and enforcing safety standards for tourism and protection of tourists.

69. States and the international community have already considered many aspects of safety, security and protection of tourism to which effect appropriate legislation has been enacted. However, not all the aspects of this problem have been taken into account, e.g., those posed by large groups (conference and package tours), special population segments (elderly, disabled, youth).

70. Tourist safety and tourism security in general in a country or a tourist destination involve a large number of regulations which should be implemented not only by the tourism administration but rather by the variety of other administrative bodies responsible for the different economic and social sectors (finance, health, environment, area development, energy, employment, etc.) and above all by the private sector.

71. The protection of human health is an essential element of tourism and its development. This requires vigorous and sustained action by national and local authorities in close co-ordination with the various sectors concerned.

72. At the international level, governmental organizations of a universal and regional character have drawn up many legal instruments, directives or guidelines, relating to the safety of various types of tourists, e.g. (ICAO—air travellers, IMO—maritime passengers), international visitors and tourists as consumers in general, (particularly WHO, CCC, OECD) or the staff employed in the tourism sector (ILO, WHO). Following the Manila Declaration on World Tourism (1980) and the Tourism Bill of Rights and Tourist Code (1985), the World Tourism Organization has recently launched a global tourist protection and security programme whose aim is to formulate recommendations to member States and the private operational sector as well as the adoption of general rules governing tourist protection and safety.

73. The failure to apply existing laws and regulations and their fragmented character nevertheless create serious problems which call for an energetic approach to the issue of tourism safety in a global and systematic fashion by all those concerned with tourism. Attention shoud be paid especially to the protection of tourists against terrorist acts and, in general, against all criminal acts of which they may be the victim, to the rights of the tourist as a consumer, to health protection and to the preservation and protection of the environment.

Recommendations

74. Legislation for the security and protection of tourists, tourist sites and facilities should always be framed and applied in conjunction with all other legislative measures designed to avoid violence and delinquency, on the one hand, and to protect and preserve the environment especially of tourist sites, on the other.

75. A specialized central body in each State should be designated and entrusted with promoting and implementing, as part of a national tourist

security and protection policy, appropriate preventive measures to ensure the protection and security of tourists, particularly at tourist sites and in the case of epidemics and threats of terrorist acts and serious and indiscriminate offences against the tourist or his or her belongings.

76. All appropriate measures should be taken to provide tourists with basic cover against the major risks they face (illness, theft, repatriation) and in particular to encourage the conclusion of agreements in this area, particularly between insurance companies, all tourist enterprises, and other concerned companies or groups, permitting tourists to purchase sufficient insurance at a reduced price.

77. With that in view, it is to be hoped that in the context of tourism facilitation, WTO will study the possibility of establishing an international insurance system enabling tourists to purchase insurance in their countries prior to departure.

78. To facilitate the implementation of their policy on tourist protection and security, States should develop, within the framework of their political and administrative organization, effective co-operation between, on the one hand, the competent departments at all levels and, on the other hand, organizations of hoteliers, travel agencies, carriers and, in general, any organization or body likely to be concerned with tourist protection and security.

79. It is important that legislative, regulatory and operational measures be taken to ensure that the infrastructure of tourist destinations is adequate to accommodate occasionally disproportionate seasonal crowds, with the attendant adverse consequences for environmental and food hygiene. It is also important, when health measures are deemed necessary, to limit their adverse impact on tourists as much as possible.

80. In order to facilitate and expedite non-judicial settlement of disputes arising between tourists and natural or legal persons, an appropriate body, such as an office of consumer protection or an Ombudsman should be created with general or special competence, to which tourists should be permitted to submit requests for the settlement of their disputes; these requests should be reviewed promptly and the tourist concerned should be notified of the results.

81. The following specific rights, as a minimum, should be granted to tourists:

   a) The right of the tourist who has suffered serious offences against his or her person or belongings to notify his or her family by the most rapid means;

   b) The right of the tourist to receive, if required, swift, appropriate medical care, preferably within the framework of the national social insurance system if possible;

   c) The right of the tourist who has suffered offences against his or her person or belongings to instigate, exempt from any bonding requirement applicable to foreigners, judicial, and in particular criminal proceedings in the national courts against the perpetrators of the said offences, and to receive, if necessary, legal aid for this purpose.

82. All appropriate measures should be taken to facilitate:

    a) Swift repatriation to their countries of origin of tourists who are victims of serious offences against their persons and/or belongings;

    b) The return of recovered stolen property to the tourist's country of origin.

83. The public and private sector should:

    a) Disseminate information to both tourism professionals and the general public so as to increase their awareness in the area of tourist protection and security;

    b) Encourage, by all necessary means, training in the various professions directly or indirectly responsible for tourist security and protection.

84. The host State and the tourist's State of origin should co-operate actively on a bilateral basis, using all appropriate means to ensure the protection and security of tourists, especially in the case of natural disasters, major accidents and epidemics.

85. In the case of serious offences against the tourist, particularly when he or she is the victim of acts of terrorism, the host State should rapidly provide the State of origin—if possible through its diplomatic or consular missions—with all necessary information on the victim's condition and the circumstances in which the act in question took place.

86. States should:

    a) Provide, whenever necessary, mutual technical assistance by sharing experience and exchanging experts in the field of tourist protection and security;

    b) Promote, within the framework of national legislation or international agreements binding on them exchanges of specialists on tourist security, particularly in the tourism professions.

IV.
METHODS OF ACTION BY PARLIAMENTS
AND FOLLOW-UP MEASURES

87. Parliaments which do not at present have machinery for the study and analysis of questions relating to tourism should envisage the creation of a specific body or the broadening of the competence of existing bodies to include also questions of tourism.

88. Parliaments should review, in the light of the findings of the Conference, all legal rules concerning tourism with a view to consolidating them (while

filling existing gaps) into a comprehensive legislation codifying the national policy and priorities for tourism. Among areas upon which legislation may appropriately focus are: minimum standards and classification schemes; pricing of facilities and amenities; protection of tourists against exploitation; redress and enforcement of tourism laws and regulations; financial incentives for domestic and foreign investors; tourist sites and environment protection, etc.

89. Particular attention should be paid by Governments and Parliaments to implementation of national legislation and international legal instruments concerning tourism.

90. Parliaments should ensure that the tourism component is taken into account when other issues of national importance (e.g., economic, regional development, social, cultural, educational, environmental and security questions) are being studied so that tourism becomes a part of comprehensive national policies and priorities for development.

91. Parliament should establish regular international contacts in order to draw on the experience of other countries in tourism policy and development.

92. The Inter-Parliamentary Union should consider organizing, in co-operation with WTO, a further worldwide Conference or regional meetings on tourism.

93. National Groups of IPU should:

    a) Bring the findings of the Conference to the attention of their respective Parliaments (particularly the competent committees) and Governments, as well as of the national bodies and institutions dealing with questions of tourism;

    b) Give broad publicity to the findings of the Conference by circulating them to the media and to the relevant professional associations;

    c) Inform the Secretariat of IPU of the steps taken and the results obtained so that this information can be circulated to all other National Groups, WTO and other organizations concerned, and to the governing bodies of IPU for their study of the follow-up measures taken by the National Groups.

94. WTO should transmit the findings of the Conference to all its member States, Associate and Affiliate Members and ensure the follow-up of these findings in the context of its regular programmes.

95. WTO should envisage preparing, in co-operation with IPU, a survey of national legislation relating to the security and protection of tourists.

APPENDIX L

WORLD PEACE THROUGH TOURISM

THE COLUMBIA CHARTER

"The First Global Conference: Tourism—A Vital Force For Peace" (convened in Vancouver, British Columbia, Canada, October 23–27, 1988):

Observes that tourism is a worldwide social/cultural phenomenon involving people of all nations as hosts and guests;

Asserts that tourism is a fundamental human activity involving social, cultural, religious, economic, environmental, educational and political values and responsibilities;

Expresses the urgent reality that peace is an essential precondition for tourism and all other aspects of sustainable human growth and cultural development;

Acknowledges that tourism is growing more rapidly than other economic sectors;

Cautions that our global society has reached a critical crossroads in the earth's history demanding responsive strategies which address the political, social, economic and environmental problems facing humankind;

Promotes tourism which is in harmony with the world's natural and cultural resources;

Maintains that the monitoring, protection, preservation and wise use of the environment and ecological balance is essential to the future of tourism;

Encourages the funders and developers of tourism projects to support development which is consistent with the "social fabric" of the host community and reinforces local values, culture and the sustained vitality of the natural environment while providing equitable economic benefits to the local economy;

Seeks to advance the full exercise of human and civil rights as stated in the United Nations' Universal Declaration of Human Rights;

Recognizes that human understanding increases through face-to-face communication and positive interaction between people, especially at the community level;

Reinforces the hope that tourism will nurture conditions through which people can coexist, share their beliefs, appreciate each other's cultures and develop friendships;

195

Reminds that tourists are both teachers and students whose classroom is the world;

Advocates the development of educational systems both in institutions and in the community, in which everyone from industry leaders and government, to individual tourists, can learn the possibilities and the value of tourism as a force for peace;

Highlights the importance of accessibility to, and dissemination of, information concerning all peoples and regions of the world;

Calls for cooperative efforts between nations, private sector companies and volunteer organizations which foster and implement places for peace, twinning of cities and other exchange and connective programs;

Notes that government, academic and private sector leaders have identified and supported the potential of tourism as an influencing force for global peace through respect for human dignity, cultural diversity and the natural environment which supports all life;

Solemnly Calls upon all nations, governmental bodies, organizations and individuals to eliminate war, terrorism and injustices, stop the arms race, free hostages and shape new policies to guide public and private sector initiatives to build a world which works for everyone, and in which tourism:

- promotes mutual understanding, trust and goodwill;
- reduces economic inequities;
- develops in an integrated manner with the full participation of local host communities;
- improves the quality of life;
- protects and preserves the environment, both built and natural, and other local resources;
- contributes to the world conservation strategy of sustainable development

Resolves to implement the Conference recommendations and initiatives through responsible action undertaken:

- individually, through our interrelated roles as tourists, hosts and world citizens, guided by the "Credo of the peaceful Traveler;"
- collectively, through the International Institute for Peace through Tourism and the Columbia Club and through other such strategies required to reach the goal of "World Peace Through Tourism."

INDEX